With best wishes from Anna

About the Author

Anna Nolan is a Polish linguist, educationalist, author and satirist with a penchant for irreverent satire and comic verse, humour being in her DNA. Besotted with the English language, Anna worked as a teacher of English, broadcaster at the BBC, manager of public examinations and developer of national qualifications in both England and Scotland. Now retired, she writes, climbs Lakeland mountains and leads a walking group.

More LAKELAND LARKS, LAUGHTER *and* LUNACIES

ANNA NOLAN

The Book Guild Ltd

First published in Great Britain in 2024 by
The Book Guild Ltd
Unit E2 Airfield Business Park,
Harrison Road, Market Harborough,
Leicestershire. LE16 7UL
Tel: 0116 2792299
www.bookguild.co.uk
Email: info@bookguild.co.uk
X: @bookguild

Copyright © 2024 Anna Nolan

The right of Anna Nolan to be identified as the author of this
work has been asserted by them in accordance with the
Copyright, Design and Patents Act 1988.

All rights reserved. No part of this publication may be
reproduced, transmitted, or stored in a retrieval system, in any form or by any means,
without permission in writing from the publisher, nor be otherwise circulated in
any form of binding or cover other than that in which it is published and without
a similar condition being imposed on the subsequent purchaser.

Typeset in 11pt Minion Pro

Printed on FSC accredited paper
Printed and bound in Great Britain by 4edge Limited

ISBN 978 1835740 507

British Library Cataloguing in Publication Data.
A catalogue record for this book is available from the British Library.

I dedicate this book to my lovely Skiddaw u3a Roamers.

We are a brilliant partnership:
My Roamers laugh and joke and quip;
They all hike with verve,
I see no reserve;
It's baloney – this stiff upper lip!

Contents

1. Dry January, the Central Ridge Mishap, a Pole in Britain and Our Brilliant Rosie — 1

2. Plugging a Brexit Gap, Parka Jackets, Fashion Styles and Covid Jabs — 11

3. Yuletide in Britain, the Wayward Royal and the Crucifixion of Non-natives — 22

4. The Wily Feline, British High Culture, the Partygate and Johnson's Visions — 35

5. Growing the Economy, the Chancellor's Conjuring Trick, Johnson's Bluster and the Scafell Pike Parable — 46

6. My Domestic Goddess Deficiencies, How to Use Buses, the X33 and When Things Are Too Good to Be True — 54

7	Exploring Far-Flung Corners of Lakeland, the Male Ego, Green Shoots, the Irton Pike Mishap and NHS Dentistry	64
8	Linear Walks, the Ford Trap, Eating Cakes, Patti's Wainwrights and the Duddon Bridge	74
9	The BBC, Violent Passions, Solitude, Mountain Goats and Kit's Picnic	85
10	Wasdale Head Upside Down, the Red Gully on Kirk Fell, Other Steep Climbs and the Nab Misadventure	95
11	Voting for Change, Another Car-Crash Interview, Clarity and Special Offers	106
12	Stagecoach and Me, My Guardian Angel, Adders on Shap Fells, the Other Borrowdale and the Claife Heights Mishap	119
13	My Birketts Obsession, My Lovely Roamers, Sleep Trackers and Other Gizmos and My Potassium Level	132
14	The Context, Delightful Creatures, Mum's Cattery Incident, the Missing Comma and More on My Lovely Roamers	145

15	Convivial Walks, Unexpected Animal Encounters and the Geological Disposal Facility	161
16	Disintegrated Investigators, Sliced Cars, a Reproductive Feat of the Year, Destructive Forecasters and Other Dangling Participles	171
17	The Wrong Type of Snow, Quiet Coaches, Unwanted Gifts and Christmas Carp	185
18	Murder in the Bath, Foxtrot with Charlie, English Grammar, Monoglots and Tranquillity	196

1

Dry January, the Central Ridge Mishap, a Pole in Britain and Our Brilliant Rosie

Decades ago, when I first came to this wonderful country from the then communist Poland, I was stunned by a great many things. One of them was dry January. An ardent Anglophile, not only was I already fluent in English, but I had learnt all about the fickleness of the British weather. All those storms, blizzards, cloudbursts and all that. I had even written this limerick to impress your border guards with my familiarity with Britain's Dunkirk spirit in the face of all sorts of weather emergencies.

> It's stormy: batten down the hatches,
> And firmly anchor all the thatches,
> Stockpile tins and cans,
> And make crisis plans
> Vis-à-vis plum brandy* and matches.

---

* And maybe chocolate digestives…

So, while astonished, I was delighted to discover that, in Britain, at least one month of the year was guaranteed to be rain-free. If that's not amazing, I don't know what is.

> British winter? Lots of rain,
> Which, to some, is quite a pain,
> Alongside wind, ice and sleet,
> Yet it manages a feat
>
> Which is weird, I can't deny:
> January is, here, dry!
> I could not believe my ears
> And erupted in wild cheers,
>
> Trying hard to spread my glee;
> Britons, though, just laughed at me:
> Why? It seems that some folk choose
> Keeping strictly off the booze!

Tragically, that's all that 'dry January' meant – what a downer! But, by the time I discovered the true meaning of this phrase, it was too late: not only was I settled in this wonderful country, but my lawfully wedded, Vinnie, and I managed to orchestrate an audacious escape from London to the spellbinding Lake District, the fabulous canvas for the lunacies recounted in this book. Such as this one.

"Help, help, I'm drowning, I'm drowning!" I screamed, sinking into the mud, which was patently determined to swallow me whole. One leg was in to above the knee, with the other determined not to be outdone. But who was to rescue me? I was hiking in our enchanting Lakeland mountains with my dear friend Patti (sadly, no longer with us), who was even smaller than me (size 8 max), so there was no way she could have pulled me out. In a blind panic, I started twisting, jerking and wriggling and, somehow, managed to extricate myself from the quagmire. It wasn't supposed to be like that at all: we'd had hard frost for a good few days, so the ground, particularly at height, was meant to be frozen solid. But we are talking about the notoriously soggy Central Ridge here. The Central Ridge, appropriately enough, runs through the centre of the Lake District. And it is very boggy indeed – unless we've had a long spell of drought (as I now know, this certainly isn't going to happen in January) or frost (more likely, although, what with global warming, things are changing).

In my previous book, *Lakeland Larks, Laughter and Lunacies*, I recounted my naivety in trying to traverse the entire ridge, which runs all the way from the Langdale Pikes in the south to Bleaberry Fell in the north (amazingly, it does so also in the opposite direction, but all Lakeland ridges are like that), without being familiar with its penchant for springing nasty surprises on unwary hikers. In those days, it wasn't only the section between Standing Crag (valiantly defending the northern flank of Ullscarf) and High Tove that was abominably wet. An even worse bog blighted the stretch between High Tove and High Seat, one of whose hungry peat hags was now trying to devour me.

Before I go on, though, I need a little reassurance: you *have* read my previous book, haven't you? *What?* You *haven't?* Come on… Why? How? Just a minute, just a minute, I need a moment to compose myself. Okay, so let's assume you *really* haven't: the lovely natives say that stranger things happen at sea. Although I myself don't go to sea much so wouldn't know. Be that as it may, I'd better introduce myself.

> I am Polish through and through,
> No, there's nothing I can do,
> But I try to compensate
> For this cruel twist of fate,
>
> Trying hard, under your gaze,
> To adapt to British ways,
> Which, let's face it, are quite strange,
> But I thought I had to change.
>
> To start off with, take the pub,
> Which, they reckon, is the hub
> Of all social life out there,
> But I can't abide the place, I swear.
>
> Dunking biscuits in one's tea
> Seems distasteful – yuck – to me,
> Plus, I never drink the stuff,
> So this challenge is quite tough.
>
> Queuing, though – it is the thing
> Which I practise with great zing;
> Yet, in our Cumbrian queues,
> Folk do push and shout abuse.

Chips with everything does seem
To be every Briton's dream;
All this saturated fat!
I would rather eat my hat.

Ditto fry-ups, which I hate:
Heart attack right on your plate,
But roast dinners seem okay,
Though perhaps not every day.

A full English? All that bacon
Leaves me quite profoundly shaken,
Also sausage – processed meat!
Stuff like this I cannot eat.

Now, keep calm and carry on
Is a cry to which I'm drawn,
Trying to retain my cool
Even when I meet a fool.

British weather? It's a source
Of our endless talk, of course;
Here, I'm truly with the Brits
'Cos it often is the pits.

If you own a patch of green,
You're a gardener – very keen;
Gardening? I'm no good at that:
I lived in a Warsaw flat.

As for many Britons' scheme
To go live the rural dream,
Cheer is what I do deserve,
Being forward of this curve.

It does seem that all you, guys,
Know how to apologise;
I can beg one's pardon too:
Sorry for invading you!

I would say that, on the whole,
I retain my Polish soul
But will never, ever quit
Trying to become a Brit!

Yep, I am a Pole trying my hardest to assimilate, integrate and blend, although, if the anecdotes recounted in my previous book are anything to go by, the lovely natives may keep me on the waiting list for a full nationality transplant a bit longer. After all, they persist in asking me how often I go home. *Home? After some forty-three years of living in England?!* It does wear you down, but, these days, I no longer waste any emotional energy on exasperation: I simply reply, albeit with a certain resignation: "Every day." They mean well, though.

In light of the aforementioned, it will doubtless come as no surprise to you that I'm doing my damnedest to ingratiate myself with them (i.e. you – if you are a native Briton). That's why, over seven years ago, I volunteered to lead a brilliant local walking group called the Roamers, operating under the auspices of Skiddaw u3a. Actually, this book is dedicated to them. Some of you will yourselves undoubtedly be members of the u3a so know all there is to know about this fantastic international movement for those who have finally reached their *proper* prime. Such as those good folk.

> Always on the go, in the driving seat,
> They've got lots to do and are all upbeat;
> In their *earlier* prime,
> They did work full-time;
> How *on earth* did they manage this feat?

And, of course, my lovely Skiddaw u3a Roamers are a part of this august movement. I always go out of my way to make the new ones feel welcome, inviting them into my group with this cordial greeting.

> Yes, you were right to have this hunch:
> My Roamers are a lovely bunch
> Who scale our mountains, walk our dales
> And follow Lakeland's lofty trails.

> I am not sure if you can tell
> That this does go for me as well,
> Though I can't say the 'lovely' bit
> Would be, for me, a perfect fit,

> But I declare that, in the main,
> Mine is a very friendly reign
> Because I prize my leader's role,
> But do beware: I am a Pole!

Actually, I told you lots about them in… You know what, I think I'd better stop repeating 'in my previous book' because this is likely to get wearying: there are another seventeen chapters in this one. And, of course, my esteemed Publisher's (it's always prudent to use capital letters when referring to those who hold your fate in their hands) equally esteemed Copy Editor is likely to get cross. If you haven't already, why don't you just go and buy my *Lakeland Larks, Laughter and Lunacies*: it's every bit as funny, and the paperback costs only £8.99. The e-book is even cheaper: a mere £3.99! Shocking that my Publisher has sold me so cheaply, isn't it? But then, it's been the story of my life. But if I absolutely must refer to my previous… oops, sorry, I'll just call it Book 1 (not that it's my first book by any means: I have written four others).

But maybe I'm being a bit unfair here: my Publisher, the Book Guild Publishing, is great. After all, they have taken me on, haven't they? And with employees such as Rosie, their Publishing Manager, they couldn't possibly go wrong.

> Who, at Book Guild, is in charge?
> Brilliant Rosie, by and large:
> Publishing is in her blood,
> And she won't accept a dud;
>
> All her chosen books are brill –
> Guaranteed to charm, grip, thrill;
> Some, like mine, provoke great mirth:
> You will get your money's worth!

Comprehensive contract first –
In this, she is so well versed;
Then your bio: with her touch,
A short one can say so much!

She is also quite superb
Helping with your title's blurb
And will always be quite quick
Over each submitted pic.

Then production – on the whole,
She stays firmly in control
From the start right to the end;
Rosie dear – we thou commend!

Yep, I reckon they are lucky to have her – we, the authors, certainly are! By the way, some of you might have already noticed my considerable proclivity for all sorts of asides, digressions and meanderings. Oh, and for tautology. This, of course, won't have come as a surprise to the three of you who have actually read Book 1, but I thought it would be best to be straight with you from the off. I had covered my back, though: why do you think I have included 'larks' in the tile of both books?

Returning to my rhymed proclamation of allegiance, it alludes to the rural dream harboured by many a lovely native. Although Vinnie and I are both first-generation immigrants (he's a Dubliner), we did actually manage to achieve this dream – and over a quarter of a century ago at that – after our midnight flit from London: we took a sleeper to Carlisle. The contents of our house were being transported separately in a humongous removal van – by then, we possessed more than just the one suitcase which each of us had landed on these welcoming shores with. Amazing how you accumulate stuff. But we had been gainfully employed in London for many years. Don't worry, we were entirely legit – nothing untoward: no hiding in the bushes and emerging at nightfall only. Apropos immigrants, have you noticed that the term 'immigrant' applies *exclusively* to those who, like us, choose to make this wonderful country their home? As for Britons settling abroad, they are never emigrants – a counterpart of immigrants – but always *expatriates*, although *The Sunday Times* once advertised a job for *ex-patriots*. I wonder how many British ex-patriots came forward…

2

Plugging a Brexit Gap, Parka Jackets, Fashion Styles and Covid Jabs

Now, where was I before all these digressions? Oh yes, being devoured by a ravenous peat hag between High Tove and High Seat. As you can see, the peat hag has not succeeded in its endeavours, having subsequently been obliterated thanks to a generous grant from the European Regional Development Fund (ERDF). Actually, I did mention it in Book 1. This grant has recently financed a fabulous passage there, engineered out of large slabs, so you can treat both my books as historical documents. Apropos the grant itself: between 2019 and its sad expiry in June 2023, £1.5 million had come from the EU. But, look, it was Europe's choice, wasn't it? Nobody forced it to lavish money on Britain's conservation projects, did they? So the EU must be breathing a sigh of relief that, after Brexit, it no longer has to. Obviously, our government isn't that stupid: I mean, it isn't going to waste that much money on conservation, is it? After all, it is nearly £2.6 *trillion* in the red as it is, and our national debt is growing at a rate of £5,170 *per second*. So the government has not replaced the European funding, and, as a result, our fabulous Fix the Fells programme is facing an annual shortfall of a quarter of a million quid.

But that's where I have truly fantastic news for you. As you know, I am a Lakeland hiker (you want to see my quadriceps). And Vinnie and I live in a pocket-sized, though utterly delightful, Lake District market town called Keswick. So, naturally, we belong to the fantastic Keswick Rambling Club. And do you know what happened? At its AGM held in 2023, everybody unanimously voted to support Fix the Fells financially – *unanimously*! We are only a small club, so we are not talking thousands of pounds here, but, as one of the titans of British commerce is wont to observe, every little helps. I hope this will set an example for the rest of the country: since lots of schemes are now losing, or have already lost, European dosh, it will be up to us, the upstanding citizenry of this country, to make up the shortfall. If our public-spirited rambling club is anything to go by, there is every reason to look to the future with optimism.

Apropos our lovely Keswick, I waxed lyrical about it in Book 1. But, although I told you heaps about it, I couldn't tell you *everything*; you always want to hold something back for your next volume. Publishers like to offer you two-book deals, you know. And what I have held back goes like this. A market town has to have a market square. Unless it holds its markets in a street, but that's poor form. Happily, Keswick has never been accused of poor form, its market square, together with its vicinage, boasting lots and lots of brilliant shops, although most of them sell the same stuff, namely walking, climbing and cycling gear. But that's because we are supposed to be this great big Lakeland adventure centre, and, once you have found a cash cow, you'd be silly not to want to milk it, wouldn't you? And this is why I have at least thirty hiking jackets – fifteen of them by Paramo alone. I think I will send a copy of this book to its headquarters; who knows, they might give me an extra discount, although I mustn't be too greedy: they roll out the red carpet the minute I walk into the shop as it is, which is great for my withered ego. (A bit further on, I will tell you why it's withered.) Plus, in a free-market economy such as Britain's, they keep innovating and bringing out new, vastly improved, stuff, and you wouldn't want to miss out on the very latest in terms of the jacket's breakthrough breathability, innovative waterproofness, phenomenal permeability, revolutionary lightness, amazing fit and exceptional comfort, would you? So, in a slightly desperate attempt to keep up with all this breakneck innovation, you go on buying vastly improved parka jackets. I do, anyway: when in Rome… I'm running out of underwear, though: we have never learnt to drive (hence the subtitle of this book) so have to travel to other Cumbrian towns by bus. Just for a pair of pants? Forget it! I'd rather be climbing mountains. Or writing books. But you can't really blame any of our forty-odd outdoor pursuits shops: if they converted into underwear shops, they wouldn't make nearly as much dosh, so they won't. Lucky you can't see my smalls…

All that said, I will take exception to anyone accusing me of slavishly following fashion trends – or any other trends, for that matter. I don't do slavish. Well, that's not strictly true: I do – but only when it comes to scaling Lakeland mountains. And my parka jackets are not about fashion style at all. I've already told you: they are about breakthrough breathability, innovative waterproofness, phenomenal permeability, revolutionary lightness, amazing fit and exceptional comfort, so this doesn't count. In fact, I make a point of disregarding all fashion advice out of hand. Whenever I buy any of the quality British newspapers which come with a magazine devoted to style and fashion, I immediately put it in the cat's litter tray. I will tell you about the cat in question, Finn, soon, so please be patient. As far as following fashion advice is concerned, all I can say is this.

> Colour red? It's *so* last season,
> And it's not for you to reason
> With supremacy of green
> Vouched for by *The Magazine*.

> It's an oracle on trends;
> Buy it to upstage your friends
> And to show you won't prorogue
> Wearing what is now in vogue.

> It does say (it *must be* true)
> That dark brown goes well with blue,
> That cropped tops are at an end
> And that retro is on trend.

It gives more than subtle hints
That you may go mad on prints,
Shoulder pads and turtlenecks,
Though beware of gingham checks.

More advice: you may wear black
And (rejoice!) wool coats are back,
Though I thought (save your dismay)
That they'd never gone away!

Ladies wanting to impress,
Get yourselves a snake-print dress
Which you would accessorise
With a hat with butterflies.

Guys, you won't look like a lumper
When you wear a statement jumper,
Teaming it with biker boots
Suited to your tough pursuits.

And you'll never get enough
Of chic Valentino stuff;
Ditto Prada's clothing, which
Screams, "I'm big and I am rich!"

For one can afford no messing
When it comes to power dressing;
Think dramatic, bold and sleek,
Think a look that's quite unique.

It could be that your Chanel
May just render you unwell
When you think about the price,
But they say the suit is nice;

After all, it's *so* new look
That it acted like a hook,
Although it is doubtless true
That this piece is not quite you.

But *do* stick with this approach:
You should buy a spider broach,
Veja trainers, ribcage jeans
(Which are *not* confined to teens),

Comeback flares and Gucci shoes,
Boho pieces that enthuse,
And the other stuff that's in,
With which you are *bound* to win.

And all will be fine and dandy
If you carry an arm candy
Studded with red-amber conkers…
Call this style? I call it bonkers!

Well, I *myself* may do, but the triumph of image over reality is there for all to see. *The Economist* (18/11/2023) called this trend 'aesthetics over achievement', although this august magazine was referring specifically to the most recent incarnation of David – now Lord – Cameron, summoned by Rishi Sunak to his cabinet so that the prime minister wouldn't be the only one flying around the world in a private jet. Before, however, this book gets too political (politics is another hobby-horse of mine, so I won't be able to avoid the subject altogether, but I will try to wrap my political asides in a thick veil of jocularity and satire), I'd better get back to our vibrant market square. There, I once saw a sight so rare that it took me a while to process what I was actually observing. The experience was so unusual that I had to capture it in verse.

> Shopping in our market square,
> I saw something really rare
> Which I didn't recognise,
> Even though I strained my eyes.
>
> I tried to pinpoint the thing,
> Ready to deploy a sting,
> But, alas, it was too quick,
> Though I noticed it was thick;
>
> It was also mostly black,
> Though I only glimpsed its back,
> But it also had some yellow –
> What was it: a beast or fellow?
>
> Having been myself a teacher,
> I had to pursue the creature,
> So I sprinted through the crowd
> As fast as my hip allowed,

> Searching high and searching low;
> Then, success! You wanna know?
> In broad daylight, in the street
> Was a bobby on the beat!

Would you believe it! This happened after they had liquidated our police station and all the bobbies had vanished into thin air, so my astonishment was entirely justified. Yep, Keswick had its *own* police station once, but, when they called time on it, the premises became a boozer, pardon me, a pub – Wetherspoons. Some people reckon that it's a much more productive use of an attractive building: after all, we have only another twenty-five pubs in the immediate vicinity – no match for the millions of tourists occupying, I mean visiting, our enchanting town every year.

In another vein – you will soon discover that this book is literally throbbing with dozens of veins – I'd like to offer you a gentle reminder: don't forget your Covid booster if, like us, you belong to the analogue generation. It's not easy being a part of the analogue generation in the digital world, but at least we are prioritised for jabs. Who says vintage age confers no advantages? Actually, in Book 1 I listed a wide range of them. Well, definitely two. Although Johnson & Co didn't think that we deserved any: we were going to expire soon anyway. Besides, keeping us alive was getting too expensive for our caring government. I've been listening to the Covid inquiry on Radio 4. And watching it on TV. And reading about it in newspapers: it's everywhere. Apparently, they reckoned that older people should just get Covid and 'accept their fate'. What's more, Johnson's health secretary, Matt Hancock (he of the infamous Covid lockdown grope), was personally going to decide who would live and who would die. Reassuring. And don't even get me started on the protective ring which he had supposedly thrown around our care homes but which had more holes in it than Swiss cheese. Then again, the Johnson government – allegedly 'an orgy of narcissism' with no direction, plan or clue – hadn't simply dropped here from Mars, had it? *Vox Populi, Vox Dei*. But, never mind all the widely-reported chaos, some continue to stand firmly by their man – not unlike Tammy Wynette. Although her man can't have told quite so many lies – that wouldn't be possible. So I welled up at a recent manifestation of such touching loyalty when a dyed-in-the-wool Brexiteer of my acquaintance asserted that "at least Johnson had charisma." That's all right, then. Since it was a he, not a she, there wouldn't have been any romantic undertones in his expression of fealty. But people hate admitting to their mistakes, don't they?

Returning to Covid boosters, don't listen to those silly anti-vaxxers who think that Covid jabs are Bill Gates's ploy to microchip you so that he can monitor your movements. *Your* movements! What makes you think that he would be even remotely interested? He has the whole planet to save, after all. Then again, perhaps there is something in it. I don't know about you, but he keeps phoning me about a virus. Obviously, not he *himself*, but his Microsoft emissaries continue to bombard me with phone calls. Admittedly, they don't mention Covid as such, but, when you engage in a worldwide virus conspiracy, you have to watch what you say, so they conspiratorially talk about computer viruses instead. On the other hand, they speak such broken English that Vinnie and I have decided that, unless Bill Gates *himself* picks up the phone, we'll keep holding onto our common sense and have all our Covid boosters. So we have done. Which is undoubtedly why our recent Covid wasn't severe at all: I was back climbing mountains within a mere couple of days of testing negative. And Vinnie was again contentedly ensconced in his shed with his cup of tea and transistor radio. I'll tell you all about his shed a bit further on. I was going to do this here but realised that this chapter would become overloaded with humorous ditties. So I will keep the one about his shed, and what he does in it, for where I can't think of enough comic verse to put in. Although that's not very likely…

> With Covid spreading at great speed,
> A booster jab is what you need,
> A little prick (excuse the pun) –
> That's all it takes, and you are done.

> Don't think the virus is no more,
> Don't think we've won our valiant war:
> The villain's well and changing fast,
> And your protection will not last.

> A booster, if you qualify,
> Will help you combat the bad guy;
> The jab will put you in command,
> So that you'll gain the upper hand.

There is no reason to delay
If you don't wish to rue the day:
Even if you are disinclined,
The jab should give you peace of mind;

Then you can go and celebrate
And not accept your wretched fate!

3

Yuletide in Britain, the Wayward Royal and the Crucifixion of Non-natives

I am trying to time the release of this book for shortly before Christmas – not that I have much say in the matter. These publishers, they are like Gods, and what they say goes. I am not a celebrity, you know. Yes, you do know this. If I were, this book would be published the minute it was finished – if not earlier. But nobodies such as me have to wait for months. Story of my life. Anyway, in case this book does come out in late autumn, I have included quite a bit in it about Christmas.

I must admit that it came as a bit of a surprise to me to discover that, in Britain, the beginning of summer is considered high time to start thinking about Christmas. An even greater revelation came when I realised that some of the lovely natives start their preparations in January, when they purchase all their Christmas presents in the sales. And, if they keel over in the meantime, at least they won't be conscious of all that wasted dosh. Unless, of course, there is an afterlife. But the afterlife is supposed to be spent in eternal bliss rather than stewing about wasted money. But maybe they don't need money in the afterlife at all… Anyway, at our age we may not even be around next Christmas, so thinking so far in advance is out of the question. Summer, however, is when Yuletide fever seems to begin to grip many Britons in earnest. No, not us, but even we have to admit that the decorations look very pretty, and you can't overdose on prettiness, can you? For a start, it's an excellent antidote to flag-waving nationalism, which ain't particularly pretty.

The gradual crescendo of Christmas preparations steadily intensifies until, one magical October day, we are stopped in our tracks passing by Trevor's house. Trevor lives down the road and always makes an effort at this time of year. We stand there transfixed: the trees in his front garden are all aflicker, there are flashing lights running along all the guttering and drainpipes and around windows and doors, on the roof stands a giant sparkling Santa complete with his gleaming sleigh and reindeer, two further glowing Santas carrying shimmering sacks are making valiant attempts at scaling the walls on both sides of the twinkling front door, and there is another radiant reindeer strategically positioned by the flickering front gate. Mesmerising! Plus, this magical display makes me think that all this talk about our energy crisis is overblown – quite heartening.

In the communist Poland of my youth, you had to buy your Christmas tree close to the big day – otherwise, all the needles would have fallen off. The tree was natural, of course: we didn't have enough plastic to waste on fripperies, did we? Actually, we didn't have enough of many things; that's what happens in a command economy, where the government – ours had been imposed on us by the Russians after the West had abandoned us after World War II – thinks that it can outsmart the laws of supply and demand, which drive innovation and competition. But it can't. Then you decorated the tree but couldn't light any candles until the first star appeared in the firmament. Again, there were no electric Christmas lights in those times; think what a colossal saving of electricity it was! Consequently, fire brigades had to be put on standby throughout the country. Actually, the boys were really happy because it was their best opportunity by far to clock substantial overtime. Returning to our hazardous Christmas illuminations, all tiny tots had their noses pressed against the windowpane, eagerly anticipating the longed-for celestial sign. I am, of course, talking here about Christmas Eve, which, in Poland, is the most important day of Christmas. And not only in Poland: many other European countries also celebrate Christmas then. Yet another excellent reason for Brexit, no doubt.

Then there is all the Christmas food shopping. I mean back here, in Britain. First of all, you have to wrestle with other punters to grab one of the biggest shopping trolleys: no self-respecting Christmas shopper would even look at those of a more modest size. But even the biggest trolley is no match for the quantities of food and drink you are deeply convinced you need. (Such a shame that Boris Johnson gave shopping trolleys a bad name, by the way; they don't deserve to be associated with him.

Mine certainly doesn't veer all over the place.) Once you have secured your non-Johnsonian trolley, you attempt to create a finely-balanced pyramid in it. But a pyramid is supposed to have a broader base and a much narrower pyramidion, and you spent all your lessons in design and technology messing about at the back of the class. So your pyramidion contains a very large box of eggs, which succumbs to the laws of physics and inevitably falls off, all the eggs smashing on the floor. Fortunately, only one lady slips on the resulting mess, but, unfortunately, she does require an ambulance. When all the hubbub finally dies down, you give in and summon the assistance of your spouse: in this way, you will end up with two very large trolleys, so your two pyramids won't have to be quite so high. And you will be able to purchase even more absolutely necessary produce, so, despite the egg incident, you think it's all for the best. Which brings me to my Christmas ditty – like Book 1, this one is also supposed to be stuffed full of comic verse, and I have no intention of frustrating your expectations.

> Christmas is approaching, so
> Our mode is go, go, go!
> We must buy a lot of stuff
> To ensure we have enough
>
> Of the lovely festive fare
> That imbues our feast with flair.
> First, we have to make a list
> To make sure that nothing's missed.

Nothing must be left to chance,
So we're in a Yuletide trance
Mobilising our grey matter:
Number one is shellfish platter,

Then comes lobster (must be dressed) –
Thermidor's by far the best –
We will serve it with cheese crust
(Adding brandy is a must).

Crab and avocado spheres
Always raise the wildest cheers,
And we will, without a fluster,
Purchase salmon with gold lustre.

As for tasty Christmas snacks,
You can't beat ricotta stacks,
Chocolate bark, pork sausage rolls,
Christmas crack and brandy balls.

Now come mains: we'll get *the* bird –
Fifty-pounder is preferred;
If we source a smaller one,
We will *still* not be outdone

'Cos we'll also buy a goose
(Serving it with pumpkin mousse);
Better still: a three-bird roast
Will upstage (yay!) every host,

Which is why we'll source a duck,
Common Eider (with some luck);
We might also get a grouse:
There's no scrimping in our house!

Then there's meats: a wild boar joint
Always, *always* makes a point,
Venison does go down well
With our type of clientele,

So does veal and British beef
(Roast the latter with bay leaf);
For our Fred, it's Herdwick lamb;
We must also get some ham.

So as not to face rebuffing,
We'll make sage & onion stuffing
And avoid a frightful tarnish
Having twenty types of garnish.

Now come sweets: our Christmas pud
Always puts us in the mood,
So does panna cotta jelly
(It was even on the telly).

Our festive stollen slices
Will be filled with various spices,
While our passion fruit dessert
Won't have equals, we assert.

As for Christmas Rainbow Cake,
It's not all that hard to make,
Nor are port-and-rum mince pies:
Baking ninety would be wise.

One would have to be a nutter
Not to relish brandy butter:
Extra-thick, it's always yummy,
Satisfying every tummy,

Whereas brandy pouring cream
Is a treat that is supreme;
Twenty pints might just suffice:
To run out would not be nice.

It is more than just a hunch:
We'll require Christmas punch,
Eggnog, sangria, party fizz
(They help oil our Christmas quiz).

Krug champagne is always cool:
We must source it for this Yule,
Also gin, port, rum and whisky
(Though they make our Fred quite frisky).

It is hoped that, come what may,
This will last till Boxing Day;
Wait a minute – just in case,
Let us get Alaskan plaice
And, perhaps, a keg of beer;
Here is to the Christmas cheer!

Little surprise then that you have this stupendous Christmas Day, reaching the blissful stage, in the early evening, when Gaviscon and Alka-Seltzer have started working their magic and you have let go of all illusions that you can still do up your shirt and belt up your trousers. Suddenly, you are thunderstruck by a terrifying thought: tomorrow is Boxing Day. (When I first came to this wonderful country, I got a bit worried because, in Poland, we didn't do much boxing at Christmas, although, admittedly, there would be some liquor-fuelled bare-knuckle fights – but not in our circle.) And, on Boxing Day, not all supermarkets are open. In the good old days in Britain, they used to be far more civilised, but nowadays they can't get enough staff, so, to retain those few they do have, they have decided to give them two days off. So, in a blind panic, you turn to your honey, who might even be your honey bunny, or snuggle bunny or sweetie pie or sugar pie or sugarplum or duckie or sunshine or cookie or honeybunch or snickerdoodle or, if your paramour happens to be an American (their language, like everything else, is more highly evolved), honeybun with an urgent request to Google the opening hours of all the supermarkets in the vicinity. Phew, there is one that's going to be open on Boxing Day, so you can relax again and give in to the pleasant post-Christmas-dinner stupor.

But it is with great sadness that I must report that my strenuous endeavours to do Christmas the British way, enlarged on in Book 1, have failed rather miserably. Which may well constitute empirical evidence supporting my theory that one ought to be true to oneself: no good trying to pretend to be something one is not. So, for our most recent

Christmas, which we spent on our own – we have no family to speak of (actually, we have some relatives in Poland, but we don't wish to speak of them at this particular time: the lovely British natives appear to expect you to mention only those you genuinely want 'to speak of') – I purchased two chicken thighs. But, before I dwell on the aforementioned thighs, I have an observation to make. We may possess no immediate family, but we have wonderful friends, whom we love dearly. And I will introduce you to two of my lovely Polish cousins right at the end of this book; otherwise, you might have had too much Polishness before you got there. This is exactly why I don't wish to speak of them here. In conclusion, don't feel sorry for us. Quite the opposite, in fact: whereas you can choose your friends, you have little say over how your family might turn out. Okay, perhaps you could train your husband – it has been done – but the rest? Forget it. As a result, some families may have to put up with black sheep in their midst. Even the Royals. Remember the car-crash interview given by Prince Andrew? The one he thought was a great success? One's princely judgement had always been impeccable.

> Cripes, what an imponderable
> That one *oh-so* honourable
> Should be subject to such panning;
> This is *not* what one'd been planning.
>
> One is simply flabbergasted
> To have been put down, lambasted;
> Where's the nation's gratitude
> For one's famous aptitude?

You *must* feel, deep down within:
One *can't* stay at Premier Inn –
A mansion is what one does need
(One must be mindful of one's breed).

It may be full of household staff,
But one would never make a gaffe
Of giving them a fleeting glance;
They were all naked? Quite by chance!

Maybe Jeff was 'unbecoming',
But one never saw it coming;
To one, he was just a chum,
And one *never* has been dumb,

Neither has one been a drip,
Always showing leadership.
One was, clearly, quite aware
That one's friendly billionaire

With vast riches which one saw
Had some brushes with the law,
But one must display one's grace
Ditching felons face to face.

One's weekends are spent a-shooting,
Why should this now need refuting?
And one's vivid recollection
Is of showing *no* affection.

Woking does a decent pizza,
But it's not exactly Ritz – aaa?
And so one remembers well
All the details – can't you tell?

One had let one's side, um, down,
But they really went to town –
British media (damn the lot):
They are like a juggernaut.

One has virtue – high and pure;
And to think one must endure
Such appalling balderdash
And give up a birthday bash!

How did it all go *so* awry?
One has to face the FBI;
It is as bad as it can get,
And one can't even break a sweat!

Well, at least one paid a princely (naturally) sum to somebody one had never met for something one had never done. Another thing about families is that, if you don't have one, you can just invent it. And that's exactly what I have done in one of my other books. Being a writer has to have *some* perks, after all. There is no money in it, that's for sure – not with Book 1 priced at £8.99. I wonder what price they will put on this one, but that's by the by. Actually, in the aforementioned book I killed two birds with one stone, although this revealed my cruel streak. You think I don't have a cruel streak? Everybody has one, but some people hide it better than others. Okay, you may be an exception, but you know the British saying about exceptions, don't you?

Anyway, when I first came to this wonderful country, I was pronouncing things properly: Leicester was Lei-ce-ster – not Lester. By the same token, Bicester was Bi-ce-ster and not Bister and Tottenham Tott-en-ham rather than Totnam. And don't even get me started on Torpenhow. Torpenhow is a pleasant Cumbrian village situated near Bothel. After Vinnie and I had settled in the Lake District, I resolved to explore every nook and cranny of this enchanting land. So I couldn't omit Torpenhow, could I? But when I was recounting my walk around that area to a local, he started laughing uncontrollably. Rather indignantly, I enquired what was so funny about my walk. To which he replied that you didn't say Tor-pen-how. So what *did* you say? Trapena. *Hello? You gotta be kidding!* But it subsequently transpired that you did, indeed, say Trapena. And Woolfardisworthy, Beaulieu, Quernmore, Rampisham – give me a break! People's names can be just as bad: Mireille, Schuyler, Joaquin, Aoife.

But that's where my revenge comes in: English isn't the only language which can crucify non-natives – Polish can too. So when I was inventing my relatives for this other book, I decided to give them tongue-twisting names. Not to the Poles, obviously, but native speakers of English would definitely trip over their respective tongues trying to pronounce them. And, in yet another book (that satirising bureaucracy), I christened myself Szczodra (which means generous in Polish). So that's my cruel streak revealed. But it's as nothing in comparison to that exhibited by the Polish inventor of the sentence below.

W Szczebrzeszynie chrzaszcz brzmi w trzcine i pszczola tez.

See, we can play this game too. I will let you Google the meaning of this sentence: these are not just consonants randomly thrown together, you know.

4

The Wily Feline, British High Culture, the Partygate and Johnson's Visions

Returning to our Christmas chicken thighs (good grief, how did I manage to stray so far away from the original subject?), they did make a delightful change from fish, which I steam for us for the remaining 364 days of the year (Vinnie is extremely tolerant; maybe that's why we are still married). But at least it's not all wild salmon: I can steam other fish as well – it works just the same. I'll tell you all about this soon. You will undoubtedly appreciate that chicken thighs are far easier to cook than a whole turkey. Some of you will have already read my confession about my earlier turkey fiasco, when the bird was left raw inside and we had to give it to the cat. But I haven't told you about the cat itself; after all, I needed to save some material for this book. So here goes.

Out of nowhere did it crawl,
This delightful furry ball,
Tabby, with a bushy tail,
Which turned out to be a male.

Our name for him was Finn,
And he did become our kin,
Although, if the truth be told,
He was somewhat uncontrolled.

"Puss, puss, puss," we'd call – in vain:
He would make it very plain
That his schedule was jam-packed –
Disappearance was his act.

He might slink off any time
To patrol, explore or climb;
He was artful when he hid,
And we knew not what he did.

Feline banquets he'd attend,
Suddenly our ardent friend,
But when Whiskas had run out,
He'd refuse to hang about.

Yet, he could be quite a gent:
On occasion, he'd consent
To few strokes behind his ears,
Though his claws induced our fears,

And his tummy was no-go
Whether you were friend or foe;
Other times, he'd have a nap
Nestling snugly in your lap.

After a successful hunt,
He might pull a grisly stunt
With his offer of a share,
Which we always did beware.

On the whole, it's true to say
He would always get his way,
Though we couldn't help but try
To work out this wily guy,

So we started asking round;
Bingo, this is what we found:
Everybody fed the cat,
Every single neighbour – drat!
Each of us, we could now see,
Was our tabby's adoptee!

And, even though he wasn't our permanent resident, he had his own litter tray in our house – for those occasions when he might decide to stay with us for the night. I've already explained what we would put into it: all the fashion and style magazines that come with quality broadsheets. And *The Sun*. No, no, we don't read it, but, sometimes, a person we know – in a clear manifestation of misapprehension – gives us a copy after she's finished reading. Regrettably, its leakiness is much greater, and Finn isn't a fan either.

Returning to our most recent Christmas dinner, for a little while I toyed with the idea of getting a starter, but we never have a starter, so I quickly abandoned all notions of such extravagance before finally relenting and settling on a few melon slices each. Did you know that cantaloupe has more beta-carotene than apricots, oranges, peaches and many other orangey fruit? You do now. For dessert, I purchased a small carrot cake, at least half of which, I knew, would end up being fed to the birds (we cannot abide food waste). I was spot on: hubby managed only two thin slices on each of the two festive days (you want to see his beautifully lean body; actually, no, I don't want you to see it lest you get any ideas, ladies, if you know what I mean), so at least the birds had a feast. We don't drink much – especially not since the previous Christmas. This is when I suddenly remembered that, in the dim and distant past when I still had all my own teeth, Baileys used to go down rather well. Actually, it was such a long time ago that I had to check how to spell Baileys. So, given that we were hardly going to consume anything sugary, why didn't we kill two birds with one stone and, in Baileys, have *both* a drink and a sweet? We did. Thankfully, the raging thirst and dry mouth which we developed in the aftermath of our experiment kept us awake for one night only, and the thumping headache subsided after a mere three days. Nevertheless, we resolved never to have Baileys ever again. Or at least not until we have forgotten that its alcohol content is seventeen per cent and what the intoxicant did to us, a lapse which, what with our advancing years, is a distinct possibility. If this were to be the case, shrinkflation would be our only salvation: with manufacturers busily reducing the size of their packaging without offering a commensurate decrease in price, perhaps they will shrink the size of the bottle to 500ml. Or, better still, to a pint, which is even less. Given that our Brexity government (don't forget that we haven't had the general election yet) offered the country its solemn promise to get rid of all this metric rubbish, there is every reason to be hopeful.

Admittedly, Vinnie is also partial to real ale. Just as well that Keswick boasts a profusion of public houses to which he can always escape – even at Christmas – when things at home get too Polish.

> There once was this gentleman Vin,
> Who thought nowt about whiskey and gin;
> A hot-blooded male,
> He liked real ale,
> And his bolt-hole was oft Wainwright's Inn.

Back to our economy Christmas (we are, on the whole, economy people). We could have bought some mince pies, of course – when I first came to this wonderful country and heard the name, I thought the lovely natives would eat minced meat for dessert, yuck! – but why do they have to encase their mince (I subsequently discovered that it was actually sweet) in this awful pastry? All those empty calories! Nearly as bad as minced meat for dessert, if you ask me. Personally, I quite like Christmas pud and cakes in general, but, if I start eating stuff like this, I cannot stop, so it's best not to place temptation in my path, poppy seed cake being a notable exception. After all, I have a large walking group to lead, so I have to keep in shape – still size 10.

We thus settled on one bottle of Prosecco (eleven per cent is better than seventeen per cent) and, for nibbles, an extra bag of organic walnuts, a packet of organic pumpkin seeds and a barrowload of satsumas. We did have some decorations: a miniature Christmas tree (yes, it was plastic, but it will see us out), a small reindeer figurine (I am, after all, an animal lover, of which more later) and some tinsel (it was slightly damaged, so they were flogging it at half price). Apropos our miniature Christmas tree, do you know that, every year, 1,000 people get injured while decorating their full-size version? But this will never happen to us, which is just as well. Have you ever seen an A&E department at Christmas? Particularly these days?

As far as I am concerned, however, the best thing about the British Christmas is music – all those cheery songs! I especially love Slade; don't forget that, when they were in their heyday, I was still stuck behind the Iron Curtain, being restricted to a menu of patriotic and military songs, with all western radio stations being determinedly jammed by our communist masters to save us from succumbing to western decadence. Can you imagine being allowed to listen to the likes of Freddie Mercury, Mick Jagger or David Bowie? The moral corruption!

So being introduced to British High Culture was a revelation. Thus, whenever I hear Slade belt out their Christmas song, I jump up and start hopping and bopping. You think I can't hop and bop at my age? You can think again: I have a brand-new hip, after all, and may well out-hop and out-bop the best of you. Talking of British High Culture, it's not just the music – Christmas or otherwise – there are also all those amazing British films and TV shows.

My initial exposure to the latter was a complete revelation, I can tell you. Take Benny Hill or the *Carry On* series, for example. Or the chat show *Kilroy*. Incredible! We didn't have anything remotely like this under communism.

Back to the British Boxing Day (I was greatly relieved to discover that Britons didn't spend the day boxing with one another, after all), rather than executing an emergency dash to the supermarket or donning body armour in preparation for the tussle which will inevitably break out over a cut-price television set being flogged in the sales, we usually go hiking in our spellbinding mountains. In short, a total failure to do Christmas the British way. Thankfully, your expectations of me will, by now, have been lowered to such an extent that this revelation is unlikely to have shaken you to the core. Talking about sales.

> As notorious as our gales
> Are the January sales,
> Where you always (yes, you do)
> Find a bargain – if not two.
>
> Overcome by quite an urge,
> Your account you swiftly purge
> (It's now down to but a dime)
> Having a delightful time
> Buying all that lovely stuff
> Until husband says, "Enough!"
>
> Then you wait, all tense and pale,
> Till the February sale,
> When you go, with joy and glee,
> On another spending spree.

It's now March – the sale is on,
Blimey, how the time has gone.
Then it's April, May and June;
All those sales – oh, what a boon!
(Don't you love the current trend,
When the sales just never end?)

When your hubby grabs your purse,
You protest: "It could be worse:
If you think about it, honey,
I am saving lots of money!"

At which point, you hear a groan
And see hubby lying prone;
This prevents a likely scrape
As you make your quick escape
With a ponder that goes thus:
Why can't men be more like us?

I can't, of course, finish a chapter on the British Christmas without mentioning Christmas parties. No, not for us: we are too old. But you have to admire the British spirit: even in the middle of the Covid lockdowns in 2020 and 2021, they had all these riotous parties at Number 10 and in other government buildings. You know, the 'bring your own booze' one, the 'jingle and mingle' one and all the other ones all over the place. Not sure why they call it the Partygate scandal. I watched the docudrama: the parties looked tremendous fun, although perhaps not the vomiting.

'Jingle and mingle' was our cry,
And we did mingle, we can't deny;
Our Allegra did come a cropper
Rehearsing a ginormous whopper;

She was unlucky she was caught
And her deception came to naught;
But Covid rules were not for us,
And we can't stomach all the fuss.

As we've just said, we were exempt,
So what we showed was *not* contempt,
Though, with a suitcase full of booze,
We would do more than simply schmooze:

We jitterbugged and played and rocked,
Although the world outside was locked.
The folk were dying, the wards were full,
But your aspersions are just bull!

Boris was, after all, our boss,
And did he even give a toss?
With his great fondness for excess,
He simply couldn't have cared less.

Pity that, when questioned in Parliament, Johnson didn't get into the spirit of things, publicly declaring that he had been *categorically assured* that he wasn't there. But you can't fault the reasoning of the man: after all, many people had fallen hook, line and sinker for his phantasmal vision of all those sunlit uplands in the idyllic post-Brexit Britain, so why wouldn't they be taken in by those earnest – and honest, *always* honest – protestations as well? By the way, I've always thought that, if one had visions, one ought to consult a doctor as a matter of urgency, but, what with our beleaguered NHS on its knees and the waiting list for treatment approaching eight million, perhaps that advice is currently a tad impractical. I'm sure that's why our politicians keep having all those visions and things are going from bad to worse. But Johnson's were of a different order altogether. Remember those heady days before the Brexit referendum?

> Single market? Easy trade?
> It will never make the grade;
> We want deals – and that's unique –
> With the likes of Mozambique.

> Customs union? Tariff-free?
> Not with *Europe,* you'll agree;
> Donald's gonna go for broke
> Cutting us a deal – bespoke!

> We've got nothing – zilch – to lose
> As we simply pick and choose
> A most scrumptious, juicy cherry,
> To make Britons very merry.

> This will cushion every JAM*
> From a harsh financial wham;
> I've a vision – can't you see? –
> You can put your trust in me.

---

*   Remember Theresa's JAMs (those 'just about managing')? That's them we're gonna help the most, trust me.

It is clear my deal's[**] a winner –
You said *what?* I heard 'dog's dinner'…
It's unfair and it's malicious;
We'll succeed if we're ambitious;

None of us (not even Barney)
Should be cowed by one Mark Carney;
Is he British? Is he heck!
So he doesn't meet our spec.

Our negotiating team
Will deliver on our dream;
Let's hold firm because I reckon
All those sunlit uplands beckon.

We beat Labour, we regrouped
After we were badly *DUP*ed[***],
And, throughout, we held our nerve:
Mine's the Brexit you deserve!

[**] Okay, so it's not a deal *as such* but merely a withdrawal agreement (I was, of course, too busy running the affairs of state to read it, but I've been *categorically assured* that it is first class), and we still face years and years of negotiating numerous bilateral trade deals, but, judging by our successes thus far, it will be a piece of cake; you know you can trust me, don't you? Anyways, I'm with this bloke off the telly who spoke lots of sense about the benefits of Brexit: if all else fails, at least it would have made us "appreciate what we've had". But nothing will fail – not with *me* in charge – and there will be *no border* in the Irish Sea. Uhrrrr, ogrrr, aarrr!

[***] Remember Arlene? From the DUP? The one who gave Theresa a good old runaround? Ha, ha, ha, whoarr!

5

Growing the Economy, the Chancellor's Conjuring Trick, Johnson's Bluster and the Scafell Pike Parable

Given that this book is supposed to exhibit at least a semblance of balance between larks and lunacies – I'm not mentioning laughter because it's supposed to saturate every page – I'd better get on with the latter. I can't deny that being unable to drive presented me with a few challenges – not sure I see them as opportunities for growth, as they used to say in the offices of FART, a British organisation I had managed to infiltrate. Some of you will already be aware that FART stands for the Foremost Authority for the Regulation of Transformation. You wouldn't have wanted transformation to be left unregulated, would you? Mind you, soon everything will be left unregulated, but this was in the bad old days before we won all these lovely Brexit freedoms.

Thankfully, things are different in our brave new world. I understand that the government is to scrap a whole host of protections shielding EU countries from environmental degradation. Among them are EU standards for monitoring water quality. Marvellous! England will no longer be obliged to conduct annual chemical and ecological tests of its rivers and other waters. Imagine how much easier it will be for the water companies, agricultural outfits and housebuilders to get rid of all those toxic chemicals on their books. After all, they have to be disposed of somehow, and just dumping them in our waters when no one's looking is bound to be the cheapest way. Which will, no doubt, be good for growth: just think how much dough the corporations involved will be able to save by swerving all those, entirely unnecessary, European environmental protection measures. And what will they do with all this dosh? Put it into the pockets of their CEOs and shareholders, of course. Obviously, no more tax will be forthcoming to the Exchequer because the rich have been blessed with a brilliant knack for minimising their liabilities, but think of all those Ferraris, Patek Philippes and multi-million mansions that will be purchased by the beneficiaries. So that will be good for growth. And growth will cure all this country's ills. That's why it has become such a mantra for politicians of all hues.

> We will trumpet this on oath:
> We will – yes! – deliver growth;
> Growth is our magic wand
> And this promise our bond.

> Now that we are truly free,
> Nothing will impede our spree,
> But we need both brains and brawn:
> Where have all the workers gone?

Yep, growth won't deliver itself, that's for sure. But, without growth, either the taxes will have to be hiked even higher or the public services will have to be cut to the bone. Or both. And, of course, it's not just the workers. Investment is every bit as important. But private investment doesn't appear to like political short-termism and constantly changing regulations very much. Can't think why. Then again, maybe it's just a great big conspiracy. Just like the Covid one. The environmentalists keep telling us that, in order to save the planet, we actually need to slow growth – or even start reversing it – and the government has secretly bought into this notion while paying lip service to growth. That's probably it. If growth really was *that* important, why have our rulers failed to deliver it? The current ones have had fourteen years, after all.

In the meantime, we have a general election coming. (As you are reading this, it will already have come and gone – in all probability – but I don't possess a time machine which could transport me into the future.) And what is the government guaranteed to do before a general election? I'll give you one guess only. No, no, I didn't mean to insult your intelligence; I know that we had the 2023 Autumn Statement. But maybe not everyone was paying attention; after all, we have Netflix, Hulu, Amazon Prime Video, Disney+, Apple TV+, Paramount+, The Criterion Channel, Now Entertainment, Now Cinema,

Pilo, YouTube and dozens of other channels and platforms vying for your time and attention. Have you seen *TV Times* recently? So the ditty below is for those who have been understandably distracted and missed out on all the Autumn Statement excitement. Apparently, our esteemed Chancellor of the Exchequer had pulled a rabbit out of a hat. Which is really good because I love animals. I think I've already told you this – apropos this Christmas reindeer figurine. So I can't understand why *The Economist* says that Britain doesn't need any more rabbits. They really need to get themselves better informed: the country is nature-depleted as it is, so every living creature helps. Anyway, this is about the aforementioned Statement.

> We are your tax-cutting Tories,
> So you must believe our stories:
> This tremendous giveaway
> Will be with you any day.

> Nine billion is a lot of dough;
> But we are certain you'll be slow
> And not notice (this we like!)
> Our surreptitious hike:

> We have taken fifty bill.,
> So it gives us quite a thrill
> To retain a hefty slice
> While appearing very nice.

Rishi's own tremendous wheeze
Was to come up with this freeze
(We don't mean the frost outside)
Taking Britain for a ride.

If you keep tax thresholds flat,
The Exchequer will grow fat,
Which is, clearly, just as well
'Cos our debt is vast as hell,

But we cannot just come clean
That the times ahead are lean,
So we have to obfuscate
And conceal our sorry state;

The election's coming soon
So tax cuts are opportune;
If we win, there'll be no guilt:
We will tax you to the hilt!

Interestingly, a tax bribe often works because many people will have already forgotten that taxes are guaranteed to rise as soon as the plebiscite is out of the way. But I have to say that I can muster some sympathy for the politicians not telling the electorate the truth. I have an apposite parable for you (isn't a parable always supposed to be apposite, by the way?). One of my dear friends, whom I was helping to climb all Lakeland fells, needed to scale Scafell Pike, the highest mountain in England. So she drove us to Wasdale, from where the route is the most straightforward. But you still have to climb 3,000 feet. No way around this. You start at the foot of Lingmell, which, although a mere lieutenant of the Pike, overtops Wasdale Head, its extensive western slope plunging steeply to the valley bottom. But your route, heading towards Lingmell Gill, has a reasonable gradient, although the Gill itself presents quite an obstacle when in spate. You are, however, gripped by an insatiable urge to bag your fell, so you would rather expire than turn back. Remember Johnson's war cry: "Do or die!"? That's exactly how you feel. Actually, do you recall all his bluff and bluster when he was World King?

> How to cover up the fact
> That yours is a hollow act
> And to hide from others' view
> That you haven't got a clue?
>
> The solution, by and large,
> Is the mantra 'turbocharge',
> Which you mouth – and with no breaks –
> While you're scoffing all the cakes,
>
> And, whatever else you try,
> Just keep saying, "Do or die,"
> Use all bluff that you can muster:
> There's no substitute for bluster!

We thus turbocharge our ascent of Scafell Pike, tackling the watery obstacle with grim determination. Thankfully, we don't die in the process. It helps, of course, that the well-trodden Brown Tongue route is largely stepped and poses no further difficulties. As you climb, you are awed by the precipitous wall of Scafell towering ahead and formed from formidable crags, on which many a climber has, tragically, come a cropper. And on the other side of Mickledore soars the equally vertiginous western slope of Scafell Pike, whose ragged contour is sharply delineated against the blue sky. No, you don't want to climb the Pike in bad weather – trust me. I know, I know, many do, but that's why Wasdale Mountain Rescue receive so many callouts. So I'm sure you wouldn't do it.

Finally, you reach Lingmell Col, a high pass between your objective and Lingmell. And that's exactly where my friend and I are now. Although we are at an altitude of some 2,400 feet, there is, clearly, more ascending to be done. She cranes her neck skyward, surveys the massive craggy slope rising ahead of us and asks me how much more climbing there is still to do. To which I pose the following two questions.

"Do you want me to tell you the truth, or should I buoy you up?"
"The truth, please."
"About 800 feet."
"Oh no, you shouldn't have told me this!"

So you see, people want the truth – but only if it's palatable. If it isn't, they won't vote for you – if you are a politician, that is. And the country is in a real pickle, so be my guest and tell folk the truth. This is why I wouldn't use any political party's election manifesto to line Finn's litter tray: while he just about tolerates having *The Sun* in there, he does draw the line at party manifestos. So they go straight into the recycling bin: I've read enough fiction to last me a lifetime.

My goodness, how did this digression veer so far off course? Actually, like my Wainwright-bagging friend and I, it still has a bit further to go because I haven't yet explained about the 'foremost'. As in the Foremost Authority. I'm sure you'll agree that any authority worth its salt ought to be foremost. I mean, would you want to work for any bog-standard authority? Unless, that is, it allowed you to work entirely from home – or, better still, from the Bahamas – and to attend the office four times a year only, but our authorities don't seem too keen. Can't think why. As it was, our Foremost Authority found it hard to recruit staff. Why do you think they employed *me*?

6

My Domestic Goddess Deficiencies, How to Use Buses, the X33 and When Things Are Too Good to Be True

Now, where was I before I launched into all these philosophically political – or was it politically philosophical – asides? Oh yes, how to deal with the challenges of getting to the most remote corners of the Lake District, tantalisingly hiding behind high mountain ranges, with no access to a car? I briefly considered swapping husbands: Vinnie can't drive either, and wouldn't it be nice to be married to someone able to deliver me to all those tempting far-flung places? But I quickly abandoned the idea: what if this brand-new, splendidly motorised, husband expected me to be a domestic goddess? Or even just to be able to steam something else apart from fish and vegetables for dinner? Or, worse still, to roast? Or, *heaven forfend*, to bake! No, this didn't bear thinking about, so I needed Plan B.

Before, however, I get to Plan B, you have to agree that at least I admit to my shortcomings. *What?* What do you mean I couldn't hide them if I tried? That's a little unkind. Look, not everyone is aware of my deficiencies in the domestic goddess department, so there is a certain amount of bravery in the ditty below. But we, Poles, are renowned for our courage. You just have to read the history of World War II – even an abbreviated version. Or familiarise yourselves with how, in the twentieth century, we threw off the shackles of our Russian oppressors, joyously rejoining the western community of free countries. Or recall how we, the Poles in Britain, have gutsily stepped in to fill all those lowly jobs for which the lovely natives consider themselves too highly evolved. Admittedly, this pluckiness is much less in evidence now because the Brexit vote precipitated quite an exodus, but you still have me – although this guy has recently ordered me to bugger off back to my *own* country after I asked him politely to dismount from his bike on a narrow footbridge. And, since you are stuck with me, I'd better come clean about my domestic goddess deficiencies.

> I've a secret that's quite murky:
> I have never stuffed a turkey,
> Neither have I plucked a goose
> Or created pumpkin mousse;
>
> As regards my pie and mash,
> When I tried, it was a crash;
> My first ever shepherd's pie
> Was quite burnt, I can't deny,

Yorkshire pud just wouldn't rise,
Thwarting my repeated tries,
And your famous spotted dick
Made my visitors quite sick;

Tatties? An off-putting mush,
Whose reminder makes me blush,
Whereas chicken casserole
Was a failure – on the whole.

Chips? No, never – with no dish!
But at least I'm good at fish,
Which I generally steam:
Salmon, haddock, cod and bream.

Sobbing is what I must now stifle:
You remember my vile trifle?
Cake was fine, however custard
Simply wouldn't cut the mustard.

Apropos my Eton Mess –
Well, I reckon you can guess,
But I do reject all blame:
It lived up to its foul name!

I could rabbit on an on,
But you'd only wince and yawn;
Let me leave you with this thought:
Cooking is, to me, quite fraught.

Now that I've been as open, honest and straight (my proclivity for tautology hasn't lost any of its intensity since Book 1) with you as our politicians – well, okay, maybe just the one – I can move on to my Plan B, which involved no new husbands. But it had to involve something, and that something was public transport. I've already told you – you know where – that even a country as wedded to the car as Britain couldn't do without at least *some* public transport. And because we in Lakeland get swamped, I mean visited, by all those lovely tourists, ours isn't too bad – particularly in the summer season. Yes, you have to plan your connections with military precision, get up at the crack of dawn and then time yourself throughout your adventurous hike to make sure you make the last bus – or train – for which you often have to sprint at the end, but you can certainly get about. For me, of course, using public transport has been a way of life for as long as I can remember: not many people drove in the Poland of my youth, and, in London, one would have needed to take leave of one's senses to commute to work by car. But, in Britain, despite the protestations of the environmental lobby, the car still reigns supreme. Well, it has to: outside honeypots such as ours, my unmotorised fellow sufferers would be stuffed without it. But you can't accuse our local authorities of not making an effort to entice the general populace onto public transport (such as it is): one had even published a helpful leaflet aiming to educate it in how to use buses. When I read about it, I couldn't stop laughing – until I was walloped by a rather unpleasant realisation that I had missed out on a juicy commission there: what I don't know about the use of public transport is not worth knowing. Never mind, there might be other opportunities to monetise my expertise, although my upbringing in the communist Poland failed to imbue me with the western knack for monetising things. I imagine the leaflet in question went something like this.

> Like your car, a bus has wheels
> (That's a feature which appeals);
> It is big, so other folk,
> Like this lady and this bloke
>
> And all others, can get on;
> It then starts and it is gone,
> Taking you where you must go,
> Although it is rather slow
>
> Because it does stop *en route*,
> But this fault is not acute.
> Doors will function just the same
> (Yep, the clue is in the name),
>
> Ditto windows, though their grime
> Makes your travelling sub-prime
> And is not what you would like,
> But the cleaners are on strike.
>
> Seating's fine, but be advised:
> Not all folk are civilised –
> When some see a facing seat,
> It is where they'll put their feet.

> One big difference can be felt:
> You won't have a safety belt.
> But our buses, on the whole,
> Do fulfil their public role,
> So, a few odd blips aside,
> Do enjoy your merry ride.

And I've certainly had more than my fair share of merry Lakeland rides. Some of the merriest involved this fantastic bus running all the way from Penrith to Ravenglass via Keswick, Ambleside and Coniston – albeit only on weekends during the summer season. But still: beggars can't be choosers. Some ten years ago now, our government must have found some loose change at the back of the sofa and, in a careless moment of distraction (there must have been footy or rugby on TV), decided to subsidise a few extra Lakeland buses so as to ease congestion on our clogged roads. And one of them was this amazing X33!

As for Ravenglass itself, it is a picturesque coastal village, sitting at the estuary of three rivers: the Esk, Mite and Irt. It used to be an important naval base for the Romans and boasts the impressive remains of the Roman Bath House, Roman Fort and other interesting Roman ruins. As well as public toilets. No, they are not Roman relics but are as rare – if not rarer, actually. Certainly now. Do you realise that, in just over a decade, Britain has lost nearly sixty per cent of its public toilets? Because of the austerity-era budget cuts, local authority expenditure on public loos has halved since 2010. Ours, in the Lake District, haven't been spared the axe: why do you think our bushes exude this peculiar odour (to put it politely)? Just as well that the human sense of smell is vastly inferior to that of canines, whose olfactory system is far more highly developed than ours. Let alone that of aardvarks. Did you know that aardvarks have the highest number of olfactory turbinal bones of any mammal? You do now.

> We may have bewitched UNESCO
> But we have to go *al fresco*:
> Without giving an excuse,
> They've abandoned our loos.

> Cross our legs? Well, for so long,
> Then the urge just gets too strong:
> If one cannot find the loo,
> What is one supposed to do?

> Although it's a splendid nation,
> It neglects its sanitation;
> Our need is existential:
> This provision is essential!

Returning to this marvellous X33, the government, sadly, soon realised its folly, and the bus was no more, but these few summers were a real treat. Now, all that is left are my precious memories – and my heartfelt ode to it, written when it was opening up new horizons to us, the unmotorised. Actually, not only the unmotorised. Don't forget that, when you use a car, you can't do linear walks. But, when you travel by public transport, you can do lots and lots of such hikes, rambles and strolls. Besides, you'll be saving the planet. So perhaps you could get yourself this leaflet on how to use buses. Or just read my rhymed instructions. Anyway, here is my paean to the late, and sorely missed, X33.

> "What's this bus?" I hear you ask.
> How about this little task?
> What will, without any hassle,
> Take you to Muncaster Castle?

> What will make you rapt and chatty
> 'Cos you're going on La'al Ratty?
> Ravenglass is in your sights?
> Or Black Combe and its delights?

> The Old Man's stupendous ridge?
> Torver, Broughton, Duddon Bridge?
> This bus is your gateway
> To a most amazing day.

> Penrith is from where it starts,
> Then from Keswick it departs,
> Going south to Ambleside
> On a very scenic ride,

> After which, it does turn west,
> Showing Lakeland at its best
> As it heads towards the coast,
> Where you'd want to be the most.

> Which bus leaves you thus enthralled?
> The X33 it's called!
> Will it stay with us for good?
> We are adamant it should,
> But some things that are first-class
> May be just too good, alas.

Sadly, my premonition was correct. In general, I am deeply sceptical of everything which appears too good to be true. Such as all the Brexit promises made before the referendum. Or all the incredible bargains you are supposed to be able to bag in the never-ending sales. Or all these advertisements popping up all over the place and pushing unique opportunities to invest in a planned condominium in Rwanda (it's a safe country, after all, and the condominium should be completed by 2050 at the latest), a lithium mine in Mexico or a rainforest in Brazil. You want to supplement your pension, right? And what are you getting from your bank? A measly five per cent. If you are fortunate. So you thank your lucky stars and jump in before the unique, and strictly time-limited, opportunity vanishes in a puff of smoke. You know what happens next – but then it's too late.

> This will be your lucky break,
> But do hurry, for Pete's sake:
> This investment is unique
> If it's interest you seek.

With a bank, you must lament
Your abysmal five per cent,
Our scheme, though, is foolproof:
Profit's going through the roof!

We've this forest overseas
Which has lots and lots of trees;
Precious timber – high in price;
Join us quickly or no dice.

If you do, then, with no trouble,
All your dosh will quickly double
While you sit and just relax
And not worry about tax.

A bank transfer would be best,
(We will handle all the rest);
Your bank details – click this link –
It's far easier than you think.

Now the scheme is good to go:
We have just received your dough,
And, in planning an expansion,
We are off to buy a mansion!

7

Exploring Far-Flung Corners of Lakeland, the Male Ego, Green Shoots, the Irton Pike Mishap and NHS Dentistry

Returning to this fabulous X33, I was a regular while it was running. In fact, there was a small group of us, dedicated hikers, who were its faithful users and who formed a delightful social circle aboard. For years after the bus's demise, we kept bumping into one another on the fells, reminiscing about all the fabulous hikes the service had enabled us to do. There was, however, one snag: woe betide those who missed the return bus – there was only one daily journey there and one daily journey back – so if you missed the Sunday return, your rescue wouldn't arrive until the following Saturday. Did this deter me, though? Did it heck.

Five hours isn't very long, but if that's your lot, that's your lot. The X33 would disgorge its cargo at Ravenglass at 11am, and if you weren't back for 4pm, tough luck: it wouldn't wait for you. Then again, a hiker of my fitness and foolhardiness could do lots in five hours. Although Irton Pike is merely an outlying fell, to get there with no car was, to me, a treat. You see, I don't need to cross continents in search of thrills: I can find enough right on my doorstep. Such as this one.

You could start at Ravenglass (having availed yourself of its splendid public conveniences first) and then follow the interesting, relatively unfrequented, route hugging the foothills of the delightful Muncaster Fell, which guards the entry to the equally enchanting Eskdale. Part of the route traces the line of La'al Ratty – the famous narrow-gauge heritage railway running from Ravenglass to Dalegarth in Eskdale – so, if the miniature train passed you, you could exchange cheery waves with its obligatorily merry passengers. You would then head for the wooded Irton Park and climb the similarly afforested Irton Pike. And that's what I did, meandering across the area and, after scaling the Pike, trying hard not to tumble head down its exceedingly steep southern slope. But then, I had to return to Ravenglass. Of course. Among all the trees, it wasn't all that easy to discern the right direction, and all I was using for navigation was a paper map: I couldn't even use a compass (I still can't). And, as a fully paid-up member of the analogue generation, I possessed no electronic gizmos of any description (I still don't).

Apropos using a compass, I have a little story for you. Keswick is surrounded by magnificent fells, sharing our delightful valley with a beautiful lake, Derwentwater. Hang on, hang on, I can't possibly get going with the tale before reflecting on the charms of the valley itself. Or at least on one of them: the lovely flowers adorning it. They have struck an accord with one another as to when to grace Mother Earth to our delectation and are sticking with it. If only different countries could cooperate in a similar vein…

   Snowdrops, delicate and pale,
   Carpet the entire vale
   As the winter, now apace,
   Loosens its robust embrace.

   Milder weather drawing near,
   Crocuses will soon appear –
   Purple, lilac, orange, white,
   They are an enchanting sight;

   And when daffs erupt, we'll all
   Watch their gleeful dance – in thrall;
   May means bluebells, and their hue,
   Often called electric blue,

   Will entrance you, make you swoon
   As they drape their fine festoon
   Right across sun-dappled glades,
   Where they vie with verdant blades.

   Later, summer blooms galore
   Will delight you even more,
   Their sweet scent (beyond compare)
   Wafting gently in the air.

All this riot, day by day,
Simply takes one's breath away;
It's a wildly joyous fest:
Mother Nature at her best!

Right here, on our doorstep! Why would you want to go traipsing around the world? Especially if, like me, you have already lived in three capital cities of Europe?

On with my story. It's mandatory for each beautiful lake to be encircled by a path so that all manner of folk can enjoy it. Naturally, Derwentwater is. One late afternoon, when evening shadows were settling over the now peaceful valley (it isn't quite so peaceful during the day, though) and shapely reflections of the surrounding fells were lengthening on the smooth surface of the lake, I was following this path to return home from one of my marathon mountain hikes. Less than a mile away from Keswick, I saw a couple walking in the opposite direction. It was getting rather late, so I couldn't help wondering why they were starting their walk at this time. After I stopped to chat to them, the guy said that they were returning to Keswick. To which I replied that they were actually walking *away* from Keswick. This was met with earnest protestations on the part of the chap, who declared: "Look, I'll show you." He then quickly opened his map, pulled out his compass, placed it on the map and triumphantly announced: "See, this is where Keswick is; we are walking *towards* Keswick."

Trying hard not to chuckle, I didn't bother to look at his compass and calmly repeated my earlier message, reinforcing it with an assurance that, since I had actually lived in Keswick for many years, I knew *exactly* where it was, and would they like to follow me. The lady immediately agreed, but the guy looked at me very suspiciously and refused to budge. Coaxed by his partner, he finally relented, and the three of us soon reached our destination. But, while the lady and I had chatted amiably all the way, the bloke had walked in stony silence, his face as black as thunder. Male ego, eh?

> The male ego is quite brittle,
> It would not withstand a skittle;
> Mine's been battered, thumped and bruised
> With each book that's been refused;
>
> It's now shrunk, but I must say
> I get cheerier by the day;
> If you cut yours down to size,
> You will be much happier, guys!

There is no doubt that, after all those rejections from literary agents and book publishers, my ego is now the size of a pea. Max. Which is not necessarily a bad thing, though. But the rejections themselves were painful. Then again, it was my own stupid fault: who, in Britain, would want to read about English grammar? Obviously, to a non-native speaker such as me, there can hardly be a more fascinating topic. Besides, English grammar has been my all-consuming passion ever since I can remember, so writing about it – albeit in a jocular manner (I'm a satirist, after all) – seemed the most natural thing imaginable. But I was no longer in Poland, and the Brits were simply not interested. So be it. (Apologies to those who have read Book 1, where I first made this startling confession.)

I am, however, about to get my own back. In this book. What I'm going to do is continue, entirely innocently, for a few more chapters, and then – wham! The wham will take the form of a chapter on dangling participles, a grammatical error which often has hilarious consequences. Over many years of assiduous linguistic research, I have collected hundreds of unintentionally funny examples and promise to give you the best. I might also slip in a few other grammatical observations, but I will try to do so surreptitiously in the hope that you won't notice. Until you've actually read them, but then it will be too late!

Now, where was I before my profound philosophical and linguistic digressions? Oh yes, on this path somewhere in the middle of the wooded Irton Park. The path looked promising, but not everything which looks promising subsequently fulfils its promise. You only need to look at our current situation. You are bound to remember that, in 2016, they promised us that productivity would go through the roof, growth would explode, prices would be way lower, the NHS would thrive (the very last NHS dentist in our county has just gone private, Cumbria joining the ranks of 'dental deserts'), the care sector would be rejuvenated (though not, perhaps, its inmates), other public services would flourish, our borders would be taken full control of, immigration would fall to tens of thousands max (it might even go down to net zero) and we would all be levelled up good and proper. And look at the country now.

They all promise us green shoots,
Sprouting briskly from their roots,
And we can't contain the urge
To observe what will emerge.

Yet those roots seem strangely stuck,
So we may be out of luck;
We must find what this plant is:
We could put it in a quiz

'Cos its progress is so slow
And it never seems to grow;
Finally, it dawns on us:
It's recovery – discuss!

Yep, those green shoots of recovery never seem to blossom into anything substantial, their growth permanently stunted. Well, certainly in the past decade or so. But promises are cheap.

Anyway, I'm speeding along this path – the time is pressing on, after all – but the trees are getting denser and denser, and the path is growing narrower and narrower. Suddenly, the trees close up, and the trail peters out completely. What do I do now? I don't think I have the time to retrace my steps so decide to press on. Not a good idea. I'm having to fight tree branches obstructing my way and to keep unhooking my trousers from the prickly bushes determined to cling to them. Then, what the hell is this? An old, moss-clad, stone wall completely blocking my way. I stumble along it to try to find a chink in its armour, but there is none. So I stumble in the other direction, hoping that there might be a passage there. Nope. But I *must* extricate myself somehow! Could I actually clamber over it? I spot a slightly lower section and decide to take a chance. My boots are slipping off the wet moss clinging to the stones (the woodland was so dense there that the forest floor wouldn't get any sunlight and, consequently, was quite wet, with large patches of damp moss colonising the ground), but, finally, I manage to get some purchase and end up with my tummy on top of the wall: nobody in their right mind would have attempted to actually *stand* on it. Then again, you would be entirely justified in enquiring if I was actually in my right mind.

Then came the manoeuvre requiring me to transfer my legs from one side of the wall to the other and, on this other side, to try to find a protruding stone on which I might be able to rest my foot. There isn't anything obvious, but, if I clutch the wall firmly enough (if I had been competing in a wall-clutching competition, I would undoubtedly have scooped the first prize), I might just be able to lower myself sufficiently to execute a jump. I do – and end up in a bog, surreptitiously concealed underneath a mixture of tussocky grass, moss and a layer of rotting leaves. Horrible! I use my sticks to prop myself up and try to pull my legs out of the quagmire. I'm not sure if you have noticed that I am a walking Pole who uses two walking poles – a joke which some natives fail to grasp when I spring it on them unexpectedly, but then most of my jokes seem to require an interpreter – yet another of those culture clashes which have blighted my life in this wonderful county. Thankfully, I do manage to reach some firmer ground, but it is now abundantly clear that I have no chance of returning to Ravenglass in time to catch my bus. I am, however, past caring: I just want to emerge into the open so that I can see where I am.

Finally, the trees thin out, and I catch a glimpse of a minor road and, right by it, a small clearing. And in this clearing are two parked cars – my only hope. Better still, one is being approached by a couple, and, much as I hate asking for lifts, I simply have no choice. So I make a beeline for them and humbly ask if, by any chance, they are heading in the direction of Ravenglass. As it happens, they are not, but, on hearing about my predicament, they generously offer to drive me there. I make it just in time for my return bus and will remain forever grateful to those lovely people. If, by any chance, you are reading this, you know who you are, although it has now been ten or so years. Thank you!

Before I finish this chapter, do you remember what I told you about our NHS dentist several pages back? Yep, it had just gone private, thus making Cumbria yet another dental desert. And just a few days later, on 5th February 2024, we all witnessed the sorry spectacle of people queueing up for hours to register with the only dental practice in Bristol which had opened its doors to new NHS applicants. The queue formed at 4am, with some people waiting until 6pm to get to the front. Unsurprisingly perhaps, scuffles broke out, and the police had to be summoned to calm things down. Welcome to the reality in our promised land. They didn't tell us any of this in 2016, did they?

Early morning, four o'clock:
Folk are queueing round the block,
And the line just grows and grows;
How bad will it get? Who knows?

Two miles, three miles, four miles long,
It has now become a throng:
Mass of people, like a shoal,
All united in one goal.

What is it? It's hard to say,
But those folk are here to stay,
So, to help them keep the peace,
We have summoned the police,

Strong, and focused like a laser,
Who have even brought a taser.
Nine o'clock – is it a stir?
Something's ready to occur?

Yep, the line does move – at last!
No, it isn't very fast,
But folk do progress, each step
Boosting their morale and pep.

All those hours spent outside,
Why? I'm truly mystified.
Are you saying you can't guess?
For a dentist – NHS!

8

Linear Walks, the Ford Trap, Eating Cakes, Patti's Wainwrights and the Duddon Bridge

Talking about delightful linear walks – albeit those with a twist (an untwisted walk wouldn't have made it into this book) – how about this one? Patti and I would use the X33 to get to the hard-to-reach and thus rarely climbed outlying fell called Black Combe, whose imposing bulk commands the south-western corner of Lakeland, majestically rising over the glittering Irish Sea. The lovely driver let us off near Whicham church just outside Silecroft, and we climbed the fell along the comfortable bridleway which A. Wainwright describes as 'the most delectable of Lakeland fell paths'. The summit is a superb viewpoint, its 360-degree panorama taking in the sweep from the faintly outlined hills of Southern Scotland through the clearer, and entirely unmistakable, silhouette of the Isle of Man to Walney Island in the south, with the unobstructed skyline to the north and east dominated by several lofty mountain ranges, the Scafell to Bowfell one prominent among them.

Having feasted our eyes on the unforgettable sight, we followed the easy ridge path to Whitecombe Head before bravely tackling the swampy slope falling gently, though squelchingly, away to Corney Fell Road. The minor road then conveyed us down the fellside, and then, equally quickly, we made our way to Waberthwaite. Although we could have caught our return bus there, we still had some time left, and I was gripped by exploratory fervour – my hallmark. Unlike me, Patti was a well-rounded human being but decided to play along nevertheless. On the map, the passage to Ravenglass, clearly marked in green, looked really interesting, so now was my opportunity to try it. Everything went well till we reached Waberthwaite Hall. Now, where is this bridge? When you look at the map and see a green trail crossing a river, you expect to see a bridge there. No, not on the map – on the ground. But there was no bridge. We walked left along the riverbank – belonging to the River Esk, which was very wide and fast-flowing at this point – then we walked right, but there simply was no passage we could have made use of. What were we to do?

We were standing there deliberating, with me peering at my trusty Ordnance Survey map, map-reading being my task on our walks. Suddenly, I noticed the word 'ford' right by where the bridge should have been. Now, English is my great passion, and I started learning it in Poland at the tender age of seven (my late mum was a teacher of English). Yet, despite more than fifty years of assiduous study of the language and decades spent living in England, I had somehow failed to grasp the meaning of this word.

When I asked Patti and heard her reply, the gravity of our predicament finally dawned on me: there was no way we would be able to wade across this wide sheet of rushing water – not unless we had a death wish. Maybe those Ordnance Survey people were trying to indicate that fording this river was possible at certain times of day when the tide was low, but it certainly wasn't low now. And we couldn't wait for it to ebb. So, as the crow flew, we were relatively close to Ravenglass, yet the necessary detour would mean that we would miss the return train to Workington (from where we could catch a bus to Keswick). That was now our only option, our marvellous X33 having already gone. Luckily, Waberthwaite Hall is a hamlet, and there were a few houses nearby. We knocked on the door of one, and, when a lady answered, we explained the pickle we were in. Thankfully, her husband was about to embark on a drive south which led via Millom, and I immediately worked out that his route would take us past Bootle, which, like Ravenglass, had a train station. A quick glance at the train timetable (which, luckily, I had on me) suggested that, if we left soon, we might just make it in time – and we did. Another kind soul to whom I owe eternal gratitude. And the meaning of the word 'ford' is now firmly lodged in my brain.

> You hike far and wide, you roam here and there,
> They say, "Do be careful," but you do not care;
> You had been, alas,
> Distracted in class;
> With 'ford' on the map, you need to beware.

Or take this delightful walk (for a change, circular), also with Patti, exploring the remote Woodland Valley in South Lakeland. I'd be surprised if you've heard of it. It's tucked away behind Broughton-in-Furness, a picturesque market town perched high above Duddon Sands. And Broughton-in-Furness used to be serviced by the X33! Naturally, the area became another object of my exploration, and I got to know it quite well. But maybe not as well as I thought… The X33 would park in the market square, so you'd get off and first make for the fantastic bakery, trying to convince yourself that the forthcoming exertions would burn off all the excess calories. That's all you can do: their cakes are utterly irresistible, and you know that, on this occasion, your willpower will be no match for the temptation.

> Cakes, puds, fudge, ice cream, et al.
> All are full of empty kcal,
> Yet each mouthful, so divine,
> Does transport you to cloud nine,

> So you scoff and scoff and scoff,
> But you need to burn it off;
> If you knew how long it takes,
> You would never look at cakes

> Or at all those other treats
> That one's tempted by and eats;
> But you banish all restraint:
> What do they expect? A saint?

> But then, just as you relax,
> You cannot do up your slacks;
> This is 'cos they must have shrunk:
> Your new washer? Piece of junk!

Unfortunately for Patti and me, our exertions that day wouldn't be all that great because the peaceful valley was nestled among gently rolling outlying fells, Blawith Knott and Woodland Fell among them, and there would be no steep ascents to tackle. You'd simply stroll across the bucolic fields towards Thornthwaite Latter Rigg, which required only minimal effort, before descending to the picturesque cluster of old buildings at Woodland Hall and continuing north along the gently undulating valley bottom. You could then return via Woodland and then along the disused railway line, which used to link Broughton-in-Furness with Coniston before this wonderful country became a car-owning democracy.

But this wonderful country seems to have had little choice – certainly not after Dr Beeching shut railway stations in half of England's most deprived areas. Admittedly, the Coniston to Broughton-in-Furness line closed a year before his infamous report of 1963. The report's recommendations, however, were a good example of bean-counting short-termism, which failed anyway: within five years of all the closures, the railways still had not been restored to profitability. And we could certainly do with those lost railway lines before our roads become completely gridlocked and we choke to death on all the fumes.

It's a lesson that needs teaching:
The proposals by one Beeching
Did not meet the stated aims
Quite regardless of their claims.

For the sake of short-term gains,
Dr Beeching cut the trains,
And short-termism is a trend
That appears to have no end.

Politicians chop and change
And then think that it is strange
When investors hold quite firm:
"Planning needs to be long term."

With most of the old railway land now sold off, all we have are a few footpaths tracing sections of old tracks. Not that they are not delightful: the stretch outside Broughton-in-Furness certainly is. When I took Patti along, that's where we started, walking in the direction opposite to that described above. All went well until we ascended past Wall End and were but a stone's throw away from the town, where we would be catching the return bus, due to depart quite soon. But, at the foot of The Knott, I somehow missed the gap in the wall which we were supposed to go through and merrily continued along Black Lane, Patti following unquestioningly; she didn't know the area, after all. Suddenly, I realised that the track was taking us *away* from the town. But the high stone wall separating us from our objective was unbreachable, and the clock was ticking. By the time we reached the side road leading to Broughton-in-Furness, we were sprinting as fast as we could. I shouted to Patti that I would try to hold the bus back for her (she was eleven years older than me) and put up as much speed as I could muster, reaching the market square completely out of puff. And there, already turning around the corner and about to disappear from view, was our bus.

I was waving frantically, and somebody on board must have noticed me because the vehicle stopped. When I reached it, I practically collapsed on its steps, with only enough breath to let the driver know that Patti was following. But the lovely guy was aware of this anyway because we had both travelled with him in the morning. A minute or two later, we saw a dainty figure trotting in our direction – phew! When I looked at Patti's crimson face, I was consumed by guilt, but she subsequently forgave me. This was my closest shave ever – a matter of a split second – although I've also had my fair share of misses (described you know where). Such is the fate of an unmotorised explorer of the Lake District. But, when my plan works out, the feeling of satisfaction is unparalleled.

Another Sunday, another trip on the X33 – this time by myself: Patti had only so much patience. But I don't mean to underestimate her talents and achievements: she was an excellent walker who climbed all 214 Wainwright fells and many of the outlying ones, and I miss her delightful company dearly.

> All those Wainwrights for our Pat:
> It's not easy to top *that*;
> She had given all she'd got
> Bagging the *entire* lot!

Scaling Wetherlam was fun,
Steeple's climb was deftly done,
So was that of Thornthwaite Crag,
Which she bagged without a brag.

Catstycam's tremendous peak
Did succumb to her technique,
And she proved herself as able
Scaling Grasmoor and Great Gable.

Scafell Pike's magnetic draw
Did imbue her climb with awe,
Whereas Pillar's bulky frame
Made her think it's not a game,

But she wouldn't be subdued
And, with steely fortitude,
Zeal and great determination,
Pressed on with her exploration.

There was windstorm on Swirl How,
Yet she managed it somehow,
And, when scrambling up Slight Side,
She took hurdles in her stride.

By herself, she did ascend
Haycock, Skiddaw and Great End,
And she climbed extremely well
To the summit of Ill Bell.

> There were many, many more
> Lakeland summits to aim for
> Till the last ascent; that day
> Illgill Head succumbed – wehey!

But, on that particular occasion, I was by myself: after decades of walking solo (I started in my teens – in Poland, obviously), solitary hiking was second nature to me. Just like using public transport. The northward view from the summit of Black Combe, when Patti and I last climbed it, was so magnificent that I simply had to discover where the entire ridge would take me to. Having admired the dramatic Blackcombe Screes and Anna Crag (yep, I have my own crag there, although, unfortunately, it has lost its apostrophe), tumbling into the deep-cut valley of Whitecombe Beck, I speeded along the familiar ridge path towards Whitecombe Head, beyond which lay the intriguing terra incognita. The passage towards the sprawling Swinside Fell was somewhat slowed by the marshy ground, but the worst thing was the stone wall above Gray Stones, which unceremoniously barricaded my route. In those days, I hadn't actually realised that a single continuous black line on the map signified a wall, but I have since learnt. Another barricade awaited me lower down, above Raven Crag, but I somehow managed to negotiate both, although it's not an experience I would recommend. But I was well and truly in the middle of nowhere, and it's amazing what a stimulant having no alternative options can turn out to be: you have to keep going no matter what.

Look at global warming: we know that we have no choice and must cut global greenhouse-gas emissions.

That's why we keep having all those COPs. The twenty-eighth was held in Dubai. It's an interesting concept: a climate conference being held in a petrostate. And its president was the CEO of one of the largest fossil fuel companies in the world. A fox in charge of a chicken coop. But at least they agreed to move away from coal, oil and natural gas, although climate treaties tend to be toothless. Dubai, however, certainly had enough dosh to throw a decent banquet for all the delegates. Actually, more than one: the conference lasted two weeks. It was attended by Rishi Sunak, Lord Cameron and King Charles – each of whom travelled in his own private jet. Per passenger, such planes are up to fourteen times more polluting than commercial planes. But nothing's perfect. Besides, Mr Sunak's spokesman said: "We are not anti-flying. This government's approach to tackling climate change, as we have set out repeatedly, is not about banning or reducing people from flying." Now, it must be because I'm Polish, but I have no idea how you 'reduce people from flying'. But you, native English speakers, have an in-built advantage over the likes of me, and I'm sure you will be able to work this one out.

Returning to my solitary escapade, I did manage to get myself over both walls, and, even though the descent from Raven Crag to the farm at Swinside was steep, at least there was a path there. My next objective was Thwaites Fell – entirely new ground. The map could only help me so much, and, beyond Lath Rigg, I felt lost. The hill standing between me and the Duddon Bridge, where I was supposed to be picked up by the X33 returning to Keswick, wasn't high, but it was sprawling, being dotted with a multitude of rocky knolls and criss-crossed by many trails. And I had no idea which one to follow. So it was a guessing game until, suddenly, I spotted what looked like a footpath. Like a pre-election tax giveaway, a footpath usually has a purpose, so my hopes rose. A few more guesses were required at each of the three main junctions – I had met no other walkers throughout the entire hike (can't think why) so could ask no one – but, finally, I managed to reach Corney Fell Road. The road, screened here by a dense woodland, conveyed me to the much busier A595 in no time at all, and, soon, I reached the characterful stone bridge, gracefully arching over the River Duddon. There I stood, hoping that my bus would show up. And when it did, barely a few minutes after I had got there, I was greeted with enthusiastic claps of the passengers who had travelled with me on the outward journey, clearly pleased that I hadn't missed it: it was a *long* way away from Keswick. The memory of this camaraderie will stay with me forever. And, of course, of this marvellous bus – may it rest in peace.

9

The BBC, Violent Passions, Solitude, Mountain Goats and Kit's Picnic

Thank goodness for BBC Radio 4. You can learn amazing things from the channel. I love the BBC anyway and would hate to see its demise or even mere diminution. Many years ago, when I first came to this wonderful country, I was gainfully employed by the BBC. No, not as a cleaner. I worked as a broadcaster for its Polish Section, which came under the umbrella of the Corporation's External Services within the World Service. The Iron Curtain was still firmly in place, separating the free West from the enslaved East, and our broadcasts, though determinedly (if not entirely successfully) jammed by our oppressors, were meant to counteract the communist propaganda rammed down the throat of countries such as Poland, forcibly dragged into Russia's orbit after World War II. After the West was hoodwinked by Stalin – clearly, an excellent role model for Putin. My mum, still in Poland then, said that hearing my voice over the airwaves was a great comfort to her, however crackling the sound of the jammed broadcast was. We were separated because I had been shut out of Poland by its imposition of the martial law aimed at forestalling the threatened Soviet invasion. The imperialist Russia doesn't change, does it? Pity the West has been so naïve.

Anyway, I won't have a bad word said about the BBC. Recently, Radio 4 announced the finding of truly groundbreaking research, phrasing it in the following way: "Researchers have just discovered that you can be alone without feeling lonely." If only these researchers had come to me first, I could have told them this decades ago and pocketed the research grant myself. Blast, so that's another income stream forgone! Remember this leaflet on how to use public transport that nobody had asked me to write? That's what I mean. I've already mentioned that I have decades of solitary hiking under my belt. It started in the Polish Tatras when I was in my teens. These mountains, in the south of the country, are so breathtakingly beautiful that, once I discovered them, I became gripped by an overwhelming urge to explore every square inch thereof and to scale every single peak therein. Which I duly did.

These passions of mine do tend to be extremely violent – just look at my ardour for English grammar – but it's a well-known Polish trait. Actually, our household is a cauldron of passions – no, not in the bedroom, behave! Although Vinnie is a Dubliner, he has his own. Both bedroom and passions. Maybe that's why the two don't collide in our house. Anyway, his obsessions may be sports-related, but they are better than tepidity. No, I am not for a second suggesting that the lovely natives are tepid – perish the thought! Vinnie is particularly devoted to Tottenham Hotspur, although such loyalty comes at a price because each lost match induces untold anguish, agony and torment on his part. I could never understand this bit. If your team keeps losing, just back a more successful one. This sound strategy is called 'ditch and switch'. This is exactly what Martin Lewis, the Money Saving Expert, advocates. No, he makes no official pronouncements on football but urges you to be ruthless in the pursuit of better deals. If this strategy is good enough for Martin Lewis, I don't see why it couldn't work for Vinnie. But he just rolls his eyes, shakes his head and sighs: "You will never understand, will you?"

So as to enhance his street cred,
My Vin got himself a new shed:
Defence shutting out the world's strife,
Upsets, irritations, the wife…

He beamed with elation and glee,
Then grabbed his transistor, made tea
And yelled: "This match – it's nearly on:
The Spurs are playing!" – then was gone.

And then for hours, from within,
There issued most enormous din
As Vinnie whooped and wailed and yelped,
Oh, how I wished I could have helped

But did not enter (not that brave):
The sign that guards the shed? Man Cave.
Later, however, I would suggest
An obvious answer. You must have guessed:

If you detect a winning streak,
Just ditch the team whose fate is bleak,
But Vinnie only looked aghast,
And his vexation was, clearly, vast:

"No, you will never comprehend:
Have you not heard 'the bitter end'?
I back the Spurs: they are my team,
Although they often make me scream."

It is my turn to roll my eyes,
For such defiance is unwise,
While, with my scheme, it is quite plain,
All men would save themselves much pain!

Nothing doing, though. Now, where was I? Oh yes, in the Polish Tatras. Over fifty years ago. Each morning, I would get up at 5am to catch the first bus of the day leaving Zakopane a couple of hours later and would then spend the whole blissful day hiking. I wouldn't have minded some company, but there was nobody that crazy whom I could co-opt. So I got used to my solitary adventures. As you can see, I was the odd one out even in Poland. But I never felt lonely. In fact, I don't know the meaning of the word. When you are at one with nature, your solitude is soothing, meditative and contemplative. How can you not enjoy that? Cherish even? I wonder how many years it had taken the researchers to work it out. Presumably, the longer they strung their study out, the more money they got. But they probably all had mortgages to pay, so good luck to them. And it makes me feel less of an oddball, this research validating what I have always known.

Anyway, I roamed far and wide with only a map for company. All the trails in the Tatras were, and undoubtedly still are, excellently waymarked – far better than the paths in the Lake District. Each trail had its own colour: a stripe of red, black, blue, yellow or green placed between two stripes of white. Alongside the entire trail, these signs were painted on rocks, crags, stones, tree trunks and other protrusions at relatively short intervals, so it was easy to spot and follow them. Your map also showed these coloured trails, so you didn't even need a compass: as long as you knew which colour to follow, you were fine. Not only did I hike in the Polish Tatras, but I also explored the Slovak side.

My adventures included surviving an electric storm high up the majestic Gerlach (over 8,700 feet high), where I had to discard my rucksack, which had metal bits attached to it, and then curl up in a ball in a rocky nook, hoping that I wouldn't be struck by lightning. Then, on both sides of the border, there were the ferocious trails on sheer rock faces which could be negotiated only with the help from metal steps, ladders, chains and rails attached thereof. In Britain, they are called via ferratas, but, here, adventure seekers tackle these routes fully harnessed. Not so in the stamping ground of my youth, where no similar security devices were available. You simply clutched the metal with an iron grip (the pun unintended), said your prayers and hoped for the best.

On both the Polish and the Slovak side, I slept out in the open with neither a sleeping bag nor even a rudimentary tent. Thankfully, summer nights are short, but you woke up freezing – not that you slept much anyway. During one such early morning, I saw an unforgettable sight: a family of mountain goat-antelopes (chamois), with the mama stomping her feet at me and the babies having great fun on the snowy slide. Remember that the Tatras are far higher than the Lakeland fells, so even in June and July the snow would linger in sheltered gullies facing away from the sun. And I was now looking at one such gully – and so were the kids (I mean the baby goats). But they didn't stop at looking: they would hop to the top of the gully, sit on their little bottoms and then slide down – much like human kids do on the slides. At the foot of the slide, they would shake their little tails exuberantly and execute a few joyous jumps before dashing back to the top of the gully to repeat the ebullient operation. Forgetting the cold, I sat there mesmerised, and this amazing sight will stay with me forever. Give me solitude any day.

At other times, I would sleep in mountain bothies or larger, maintained, shelters akin to British youth hostels. Their accommodation was usually rudimentary, but, in those days, my teenage bladder was more capacious than it is now, and I didn't mind bunk beds. Yep, one's bladder certainly doesn't improve with age, that's for sure. If only a bladder enlargement was one of these cosmetic procedures which are widely touted as the answer to all one's woes.

Botox, fillers, liposuction –
Here is our introduction
To the world of instant beauty:
You will get a rounder booty,

Pouty lips, big boobs, new nose
As the answer to your woes,
And we'll make you wrinkle-free –
A great prospect, you'll agree.

There is more – it's getting madder;
All I want is a new bladder!

But this is now, and that was then, so, in my, sadly not misspent, youth, I was able to explore even the most remote and intriguing parts of the beautiful Tatras, starting at the crack of dawn and not finishing until dusk. There were also some funny moments. Once, I got caught out in a downpour. Luckily, I had completed my climb and was now at the foot of a vertical wall of rock. Half-blinded by the rain, I spotted a small cave, which was, however, sufficiently big for me to shelter from the deluge. I stood there for absolutely ages, but the rain simply wouldn't abate. Finally, I decided that I couldn't wait any longer and ran out into the rain. But as soon as I emerged into the open, there was no rain! The sky was blue, the sun was shining, and the world was sparkling. I looked up and understood: my little cave sat right at the bottom of a vertical gully which acted like a giant funnel, channelling all the water from higher up and then sending it tumbling down right in front of my shelter. This, in turn, created a watery barrier at its entry, which persisted even after the rain had stopped. I couldn't stop laughing!

These few vignettes of my youthful exploits in the Tatras are meant to oil the passage to a few more of my solitary escapades in the Lake District, themselves meant to enable this book to fulfil its quota of lunacies. Some were, of course, recounted in Book 1, but there have been many more. I've already told you how an unmotorised hiker gets from Keswick to Wasdale Head *per pedes*, but I may as well remind those who haven't read the book. You get the bus to Seatoller and then spend the next three hours climbing to the mountain pass called Sty Head and then descending to Wasdale Head. You are then ready to start your walk *properly*. You have many splendid options there, which is why Wasdale's car parks are jam-packed in high season.

Mind you, all Lakeland car parks are jam-packed – particularly during the summer: after all, our enchanting Lake District gets swamped by roughly 18 million occupiers, I mean visited by lovely holidaymakers, each year. Some are walkers, and some are not, but, when you see some infinity pool or another site of interest splashed all over social media, you want to go and see it for yourself, don't you? So the traffic gets worse and worse, and our narrow and winding roads get more and more clogged. But you can't spoil people's fun. I mean, would you have the heart to stop Kit and his clan from having their picnic?

"Sun is out," whoops joyful Kit,
"Picnic's just the thing for it;
Haven't had one in a while:
Let's go picnic – yup, in style!"

Missus nods and kiddies yell:
"Picnic's, like, so cool as well;
We can have pork pies and things
Like them tasty onion rings!"

"And Scotch eggs, and pick 'n' mix,
Pepsi and this stuff on sticks…"
"I want lots of little cakes,
Them pink ones that Granny bakes…"

"Shut up, kids; it's Pimm's for me,
And this tart they make with brie,
Oh, you won't forget, me darling:
We will need a crate of Carling."

"Stop, you lot; I must insist
That we make ourselves a list."
Shortly, the entire clan
Sets about their picnic plan

In a most excited mood,
Listing beverages and food,
Nibbles, table, chairs and sprays
And, of course, Heinz mayonnaise.

Their old car, packed out, does groan,
And they've yet to load the drone,
But they manage and depart
Very chipper, in good heart.

Hills and lakes are whizzing past,
Wow, this landscape is so vast,
Kids don't squabble and just stare:
"Are we very nearly there?"

"For gossake, just get a grip,
Don't go spoiling our trip,
We want nice smooth tarmac, innit?
Wait a minute, wait a minute:

Can you see, just by this mast,
There is lots of cars – at last!"
So they pull in and unload
In a holiday-like mode.

Then, they have a lovely siesta
Twixt a Skoda and Ford Fiesta;
Kit, however, has a snigger:
"They should make them car parks bigger."

Admittedly, Wasdale Head tends not to attract this particular type of customer: after all, it's a gateway to serious climbs, of which more in the next chapter.

10

Wasdale Head Upside Down, the Red Gully on Kirk Fell, Other Steep Climbs and the Nab Misadventure

You have now reached Wasdale Head, cosily nestling at the bottom of the valley and being surrounded by magnificent fells: Kirk Fell, Great Gable, Lingmell, Yewbarrow and Wasdale Red Pike, with the mighty Pilar, Scafell and Scafell Pike close by. Wherever you look, you have to crane your neck skyward, and, wherever you climb, you have to contend with steep slopes. Of course, you could also spend the whole day sipping beer at Wasdale Head Inn – but surely not if you have expended all this effort getting yourself there on foot all the way from Seatoller.

I have, of course, tackled all the climbs from Wasdale Head, many of them by myself, and can vouch for the steepness of many. Take the one from Mosedale, a valley jutting sideways, to Dore Head – an unremitting slog up scree, both the steepness and looseness of the terrain impeding progress. Thankfully, sections of the scree can be bypassed – but no strategy can lessen the severity of the gradient. Even worse is the scree blighting the vertiginous ascent to Wind Gap, separating Scoat Fell from Pillar. There, you literally take one step forward only to slide two steps back, and there is no bypass because you are constrained by your scree gully – never again! Equally strenuous is the straight-up climb of Kirk Fell, during which 'looking backwards, between one's legs, there is a superb upside-down view of Wasdale Head', according to A. Wainwright, whom we must forgive for his grammatical lapse (exposed in Chapter 16). Grammar aside, he was dead right, I can tell you.

> Want to scale this peak – Kirk Fell?
> I don't want to break the spell
> Or to give you quite a fright,
> But you cannot stand upright
>
> On this unremitting slope:
> Are you sure that you will cope?
> This has fallen on deaf ears,
> And they start sans any fears;
>
> It's too steep to turn around,
> They are bent: it's upside down –
> Wasdale Head, between their knees!
> But they mustn't simply freeze,

And they should instead plod on:
They are simply too far gone,
Their vertiginous ascent
Leaving them completely spent.

When they stagger to the top,
They collapse and throw a strop:
"But you didn't say!" You grin:
With such folk, you just can't win!

Or take the extremely challenging scree scramble up Little Hell Gate to reach the summit of Great Gable. Hell it certainly was, and even the magnificent rock scenery en route won't induce me to repeat the experience. You could also climb Scoat Fell along the little-known, but quite exciting, Black Comb route, which traces the source of Mosedale Beck and is enclosed by walls of rock. Especially precipitous is the shaded, eastern, flank of Red Pike, its rocks being covered in dark-green moss and continuously dripping water – quite an intimidating sight when you are in this unfrequented area all by yourself.

Obviously, I have also tackled all the touristy ascents from Wasdale Head, but they will have been described in countless Lakeland guidebooks, and I have no intention of aping other authors. What's different about my Wasdale escapades was how I was going to get myself back to Keswick with no car. Challenging when you are on top of Yewbarrow, Red Pike, Scoat Fell or Scafell and not that easy even from Pillar or Kirk Fell. To avoid repeating myself, I'm going to mention only the last two ones. Essentially, your main options are to return either to Honister Pass along the Kirk Fell Terrace (between Black Sail Pass and Beck Head) and then Moses Trod or to Gatesgarth near Buttermere via Black Sail Pass and Scarth Gap. The latter, however, forces you to descend all the way to Ennerdale before making you climb again to get yourself out of the valley and down onto the Buttermere side. And, when you have walked all the way from Seatoller in Borrowdale to Wasdale Head in the first place, it makes for a *very* long day. But I have escaped along both routes on numerous occasions. And, although by the time I reach Gatesgarth I'm usually dog-tired, I can't help a little smile whenever I pass by the farmhouse there.

> At the foot of Fleetwith Pike
> Stands the house you'd really like:
> It has got a garden gate
> And a roof of Lakeland slate,
> Plus, a porch that's well designed,
> But it has no neighbours, mind,
> For the house is quite remote,
> Yet it has a sign of note:
> (I'd had *neither* gin *nor* scotch)
> 'Neighbourhood' it says – then 'watch'!

Whether I end up near the neighbourless vigilantes at Gatesgarth or on top of Honister Pass, the idea is to make it in time for the last bus. Otherwise, it's a taxi job: in Book 1, I told you all about Garry with a taxicab, so I daren't repeat myself here. Suffice it to say that he had come to my rescue on numerous occasions. But, if I am on time, I then stand by the road hoping that my bus won't be late. Which it often is:

our narrow roads can get badly clogged. It doesn't help that the invaders, I mean tourists, often park crazily: you want to see Borrowdale Road in high season. And, when I finally make it home at dusk – and dusk in summer comes quite late – Vinnie just gives me one of his resigned looks, shakes his head and points at the cold fish forlornly sitting atop a pile of soggy veggies (he, too, can use the steamer).

Apropos very steep climbs, in my lunatic period I was tempted by all sorts of insane routes. Such as the red gully on Kirk Fell. On that occasion, I approached the mountain from Buttermere via Ennerdale. Having tackled all the touristy approaches described by A. Wainwright, I was still not content, looking for adventurous alternatives. But when no alternatives are described in guidebooks, there is usually a good reason for the omission. Surveying the rocky slope between Black Sail Pass and Bayscar Slack, I noticed a gully leading straight up. It appeared just about doable, so off I went. But the higher I climbed, the steeper the gully became. On similar occasions, it's sometimes possible to retreat by using the highly-specialised technique which, in climbing circles, is known as 'five points of contact' (actually, I did mention it in Book 1).

> It can't be denied, I have quite a drive:
> When scaling these fells, I do come alive;
> If need be, I, umm...
> Slide down on my bum;
> My contact with rock? Those points: they are five!

But not on that particular occasion: I ended up in a narrow chimney which was so steep that it was obvious that to clamber back down was no longer possible – even with the help from my posterior. I thus had to continue inching upwards. The soil in the chimney was red, and, as I was desperately clutching at whatever there was there to clutch at, my hands became red, with red soil lodged under my fingernails. Eventually, my ordeal came to an end, and, as I collapsed on easier ground, I promised myself to stop similar experimentation – a vow I quickly broke.

On one of the several occasions when this happened, I was much closer to home, on Mellbreak, although this route is actually described in one of A. Wainwright's guides. He obviously didn't suffer from vertigo. I got off the Buttermere bus at Lanthwaite Green, at the foot of the imposing Grasmoor. The popular path then conveyed me along the shore of the lovely Crummock Water to the bottom of Mellbreak's sprawling eastern slope, dramatically plunging to the lake and crowned with impressive-looking rocks. My route led straight up a very steep scree slope, where, again, it was a case of one step up and two steps down. It took me ages to reach the rocky rampart at the very top, intersected by what Wainwright calls Pillar Rake, which, to me, was the intimidating part of the climb. Although the passage along the rake itself wasn't particularly difficult, the rake slanted towards the vertical gullies below, whose openings gave the impression of being keen to embrace any hiker tumbling from the rake so that the gully would then be able to convey them right to the bottom of the slope in extra-quick time. Since I'm no good with exposure, I eyed the precipice below with great trepidation and crawled along the rake with utmost care. I was certainly mightily relieved when I reached the wide summit ridge at the point where it dips between both tops. Another one-off, that's for sure.

Since we are already by Crummock Water, I might as well tell you about my straight-up ascent of the local colossus, Grasmoor, which sits opposite Mellbreak but is much higher and bulkier. You again get off the bus at Lanthwaite Green but keep to the eastern side of the lake. There are several touristy routes leading to the summit, of course, but you have passed the touristy stage and want something more. So you raise your eyes skyward and gird your loins in preparation for a vertiginous climb. First comes a steep scree run, which, however, is as nothing in comparison with what's to come. The scree is followed by a brackeny section, and then the route steepens further, the faint trail disappearing into thick heather. You scramble straight up the rough craggy slope at a forty-degree angle, clutching at the stunted vegetation for dear life. After negotiating several brutal stony gullies and an airy arete, where you are sorely tempted to close your eyes, you finally reach the rocky Grasmoor End, which signals the end of your worst exertions. But it's been an arduous climb all right. I subsequently introduced my dear friends, Bobby and Patti, to this adventurous route, although they didn't seem too effusive in expressing their unbridled delight. Can't think why. While Patti is no longer with us, Vinnie's and my friendship with Bobby has now endured for twenty years, which tells you all you need to know about his forbearance: I had subjected him to quite a few trials, more of which later.

The straight-up ascent of Pillar from Ennerdale – the hike itself commencing at Buttermere – was similarly demanding. On this occasion, my victim was Vinnie. Having descended into Ennerdale over Scarth Gap and crossed the River Liza over the war memorial footbridge, we tackled the steep rocky slope head on, emerging by Pillar Cove at the foot of the towering Pillar Rock. Bypassing the imposing obstacle, we reached the High-level Route by Robinson's Cairn before heading for Shamrock Traverse. My heart in my boots, I cleared the traverse, which, like Pillar Rake on Mellbreak, slants rather unpleasantly towards the precipice – another frightening moment. Vinnie, meanwhile, decided to climb straight on, an ascent which, according to his subsequent report, was quite precarious. My path also decided to climb up the vertiginous slope ahead, leaving me no say in the matter. Suffice it to say that, when I finally scrambled onto the summit of Pillar and was reunited with Vinnie, I knew I would never tackle this ascent again. That said, I became rather fond of the High-level Route, which doesn't lead to the top but is very interesting, weaving its way among most magnificent mountain scenery across Pillar's Ennerdale flank.

Another steep ascent was that of The Nab, a fell which, many years ago, I needed to climb for my fourth or fifth round of Wainwright fells. The difficulty there was of a slightly different nature: if you want to climb the mountain straight up, you will be trespassing. You can, of course, reach the summit from the back by climbing over the higher Rest Dodd, and I had done so several times, but the passage between both summits is blighted by peat hags and thus rather unpleasant when the ground is wet. So, on this occasion, I was going to climb the fell from the bottom of Bannerdale (off Martindale): after all, the path leading straight up the fell's steep north shoulder was clearly visible and obviously well-trodden – despite the unforgiving gradient.

There was a small problem, however: the area at the foot of the fell is privately owned by Dalemain Estate, which has a red-roofed bungalow and, I think, a keeper's cottage there. That's where I thought my foreignness might come in handy: if I was caught, I was going to come up with: "I no understand, I no speaking English," in the most exaggerated foreign accent possible. I thus took the bus to Patterdale and climbed to Boredale Hause and then to the Beda Fell ridge higher up before descending to the bottom of Bannerdale. There, I affected nonchalance as I opened the gate with the sign *Private*. But, as I was darting towards the bottom of Nab's shoulder along the private road, I heard a vehicle approaching from behind. It was too late to hide, so I had no choice but to continue – albeit nervously. When the car drew level, it stopped, and the driver wound down the window and looked me up and down. So what do I do? Instead of coming out with: "I no understand, I no speaking English," in the thickest accent I am capable of, I offer him an insipid smile and mumble, "Hello."

"And where are we off to now?" asks the guy.

"*Only* The Nab," I whisper.

"And then?"

"Hartsop."

Which was a blatant lie: I had planned to descend the same way and then to dash to Howtown to catch the Ullswater ferry to Glenridding before returning from there by bus; I had it all timed with the utmost precision. But there was no way I was going to tell him that I was planning to trespass *twice*. He had a little ponder, looked me up and down again but then let me go on my merry way – phew! Despite my tongue-tiedness and turned-down volume, he had probably detected my accent and put my misdemeanour down to ignorance. You know how it is with these foreigners.

I did bag my fell but, of course, couldn't possibly risk getting caught twice. So I had to negotiate the unpleasant peat hags at the back of The Nab, climb Rest Dodd and then descend to Hartsop, where there was a bus stop. It was too late for me to catch the Keswick bus, however, so I had to make a lengthy detour via Penrith – another long day and another cold fish dinner. But, before you denounce me to the authorities, A. Wainwright had also trespassed there while carrying out research for his guidebook – he admitted this much. So there.

There were many more steep climbs, both solitary and accompanied, such as the one up the seemingly vertical North-west Ridge on Catstycam, the terrifying Jack's Rake on Pavey Ark, the vertiginous Fisher's Wife's Rake (don't you just love these two apostrophes!) on Clough Head, the even steeper Lord's Rake on Scafell (another excellent apostrophe – I cannot fathom why the lovely natives get confused by the apostrophe, but that's the subject for another book) as well as the full-frontal climb of Crinkle Crags from Oxendale, the scramble up the scree gully by Bowfell Buttress, the perpendicular clamber along the south-west arete terminating on the summit of Skiddaw Little Man (which is not little at all), the sharp pull-up on Slight Side en route to Scafell from Eskdale and the 'on-the-nose' ascent of Eagle Crag above Stonethwaite to name but a few. I have to be careful, however, not to bore you to death. After all, you will want to know the result of the 2024 general election, so expiring before this exciting event would be injudicious to say the least, and I want no part in it. Unless the plebiscite has already taken place, that is, but I wouldn't want your demise on my conscience anyway.

11

Voting for Change, Another Car-Crash Interview, Clarity and Special Offers

Last year, 2023, was a good one: Britain managed to get through it with only one prime minister. But, soon, we will be choosing a new one, who may, or may not, be the old one. When you read this, we might have already made our collective decision, but I have no crystal ball: as I'm writing, this momentous event is still ahead of us. It probably won't come as a surprise to you that the run-up to the general election is a truly exciting time for a politics afficionado such as me. Although I am a floating voter, I know exactly for whom I am going to cast my ballot on this occasion: after all, Keswick has an excellent parliamentary candidate. Obviously, there will be several names on the ballot paper – this wonderful country is not Russia, after all – but, as far as I am concerned, the others won't even get a look in. By the way, when I first came to Britain, I thought that it must be rather frightening being a floating voter: I feel uncomfortable on water even when there are no waves. But, having subsequently learnt the true meaning of this phrase, I have become one. No, not the phrase – the floating voter. Being an outsider, I don't feel bound by any tribal allegiances, my lovely Roamers constituting my only tribe.

So, first, I scrutinise each political party's manifesto and have a good laugh. I then quicky put it in the recycling bin – you will now be aware that Finn won't let it go in his litter tray. If you saw his claws, you wouldn't argue either. He definitely isn't anything like the feline in the limerick below.

> This, my friends, is where it's at:
> They went off to sit a cat,
> All ready to test
> Their new scratch-proof vest,
> But the feline just sat on the mat!

Perhaps I should get myself one of those vests… Returning to my pre-election research, I then observe the politicians on TV to see if the words which come out of their mouth are congruous with their body language. But you also have to listen to the words themselves – even if they have been lifted straight from a work of fantasy. Which, regrettably, happens far more frequently than I would like. But I have been listening carefully to what Rishi Sunak has to say; after all, the Conservatives have been in power for the past fourteen years. I'm sure you will agree that his speech at the 2023 Tory Party Conference, alongside all sorts of other public pronouncements, could be taken as a prologue to the Tory election campaign. Here is a little reminder.

"It's not easy to arrange,
But we must renew and change;
Today heralds a new start,
Which is simply off the chart:

"HS2 has got to go:
It is costing too much dough,
But we're gonna help the north:
Housing, transport and so forth.

"Our values we'll defend:
Culture wars will have to end,
Ditto planning for short term,
Even if this makes some squirm.

"Growth will make the country rich,
(We do not foresee a glitch);
Labour hasn't got a clue,
But we know just what to do.

"Education we'll transform,
Making excellence the norm,
We'll smash lobbies, end their clout,
And corruption we'll stamp out.

"NHS will simply thrive
Once we have applied our drive;
Social care? It will be cured;
Of this you can be assured.

"Those small boats? They will be stopped;
There's a scheme that we'll adopt,
And we'll slash the country's debt –
Don't you worry, don't you fret.

"It's renewal – we are it;
We appeal to every Brit:
You will shortly have a choice:
Vote for change – let's hear your voice!"

There's disquiet in the room:
"Change from *what*, and change from *whom*?"
"We've been clear and want no fuss:
Vote for change – the change from… us."

So I listen to all of this and have another good laugh. Obviously, I also listen to Keir Starmer and all the others. I then tune into Radio 4 and watch Laura Kuenssberg and Robert Peston on TV. And read *The Economist* and *Financial Times*. What? Using social media as a source of reliable information? You gotta be joking! You know that seventy per cent of all the so-called information on Twitter (aka X) is completely made up, don't you? Returning to Laura Kuenssberg, I've just watched the car-crash interview given on her programme by Baroness Michelle Mone (ennobled by David Cameron in yet another manifestation of his impeccable judgement in his pre-Lord days) and her husband, Doug Barrowman, in which they denied profiteering to the tune of sixty million pounds from supplying the NHS with defective Personal Protective Equipment (PPE) during the Covid pandemic.

I have to admit that Baroness Mone's earnest protestations of innocence and lachrymose claims of scapegoating brought a tear to my eye: you really have to feel sorry for these put-upon multi-millionaires. In case you missed the interview, this is what she had to say.

> "Telling lies is not a crime,
> So I won't be doing time;
> Yes, Doug made a lot of dosh,
> But your charges are just tosh.
>
> "Business folk like us do know
> How to rake in all this dough,
> And upheaval is our chance
> To improve our circumstance.
>
> "Covid crisis was acute,
> This was never in dispute,
> But our friendly Michael Gove
> Did unlock this splendid trove.
>
> "Sixty million? That's not much,
> Plus, it isn't mine as such:
> Doug has put it all in trust,
> So I'm hurt by your disgust."

But our Laura wouldn't be taken in and continued probing, doing as good a job as Emily Maitlis had done handling her interview with Prince Andrew in 2019. Give me the BBC any day. As for using Twitter (I mean X, but old habits die hard), Facebook, Instagram, TikTok, YouTube, Reddit,

WeChat and the like as a source of reliable information – not on your nelly! Back to my pre-election strategy (I have been inspired by our politicians there: if they have one, I will jolly well have one of my own), a floating voter worth his or her salt also attends hustings, which is why you will usually find me in the front row. No, this year I don't have to – the choice is obvious – but I have done in the past. Hustings are usually held in church halls. Probably to invoke divine intervention – particularly if candidates are of the calibre exemplified below.

This particular wannabe parliamentarian opened the hustings by commenting on immigration. His question: "A million Poles enough for you?" immediately endeared him to me because he was clearly implying that a million Poles may actually *not* be enough. Strictly speaking, he should have said 'a million and one', but he had no way of knowing that I was in the audience. His prescience, though! Employers are currently crying out for workers. Wherever you turn, you see signs: *We are recruiting*. But, even though this took place a few years back, before the Brexit-induced exodus emptied the country of many of its most eager workers, I was impressed. Regrettably, the good impression evaporated (can an impression evaporate?) as soon as I looked at his election leaflet. I promise you that I'm quoting his manifesto *exactly* as he had phrased it: although I have been blessed with a writer's vivid imagination, there is no way I could have come up with anything remotely resembling his impassioned arguments. In it, he excoriated the Green Party for being '*venimently* [sic] against nuclear energy', castigated 'this present *governments* [sic] stopping' of various renewable-energy subsidies and lambasted the supporters of '*Jeremy Corbyns* [sic] Labour Party' en masse. He also wondered when 'the *resident's* [sic]' of Keswick would get the global warming message, implored us 'to ensure that our *ancestors* [sic] have a planet to inhabit' and promised those who disagreed with his message that they 'will *dislike* increased sea levels even *less* [sic]'. The leaflet finished on an uncharacteristically literate, if a tad contradictory, note: 'We have the 27th best education system in the world and every year it seems to get worse. The state education system has failed to produce results, so a drastic rethink is required to improve results'. How about enticing to Britain a few more of my Polish compatriots who, like me, specialise in the intricacies of English grammar, punctuation and usage? Having professionally copy-edited countless publications, including quite a few books, all littered with grammatical, punctuation and spelling errors, I can clearly see that I could do with reinforcements.

Anyway, no hustings for me this year. And wasn't it nice of our Conservative candidate to send me a Christmas card? Shame he'd never done this before, but better late than never. Anyway, all those political interviews on the radio and TV are a real treat. Regrettably, not every politician is as explicit as Rishi Sunak. Have you noticed a trend there? I think it became particularly pronounced during the reign of Theresa May, whose favourite adjective was 'clear', favourite noun 'clarity' and favourite clause 'I'm clear'. And now they are all at it. Take this political interview conducted by one of Britain's excellent journalists – nearly as excellent as Emily Maitlis and Laura Kuenssberg – with a colossus of British politics. This is what the politico had to say.

"I have been extremely clear
(Clearer than it might appear)
What our position is
So as to pre-empt your quiz;

"*What?* You say you do not know?
Such a journalistic pro?
It is clear, let me repeat
(And I've put this in a tweet)

"That our message is overt,
This I have to reassert;
Being clear is, clearly, best
Isn't that quite manifest?

"What? You say you are in doubt?
You don't know what we're about?
I refute this groundless charge:
Our vision is writ large.

"You say we are clear as mud?
That to fib is in our blood?
Look, young man, it is quite plain
That your charges are insane.

"We are a united band,
You know where, with us, you stand,
Our concordance is of note,
We are clear: we want your vote!"

So expect a lot of clarity during the forthcoming election campaign. And, of course, lots and lots of wild promises, although many of them will be uncosted. One will undoubtedly pertain to raising productivity because this would, in turn, fuel growth. There is thus no doubt that we will hear all those entreaties to the private sector to invest more. But the private sector won't want to invest more until it knows which way the wind is blowing. So it will have to come up with a ruse. Actually, it probably already has. After all, most of my time at FART was spent in meetings.

> Productivity has stalled?
> We, like you, are quite appalled,
> But we think we know the answer;
> Do you want to hear our plan, sir?
>
> It's so simple yet effective:
> We will issue a directive
> (To be savoured like ambrosia) –
> It will say it is symposia,
>
> Fora, summits, congregations
> That will form quite firm foundations
> For our corporate success –
> Nothing more and nothing less.
>
> Now it's issued – glory be!
> Let's commence our meeting spree,
> Starting with the central caucus,
> Which, while on occasion raucous,

Never fails to set the date
Of the next one – ain't that great!
The same goes for other sessions;
Fair enough, there are digressions,

But we think that you will find
We are really of one mind,
Though it has to be attested
That, sometimes, the date's contested;

We do get there in the end,
Which is why we must contend
That such a decisive action
Amplifies job satisfaction.

Meetings, meetings and more meetings,
We sign off now (with warm greetings),
For the next one's just begun;
So effective – and such fun!

Productivity? Job done –
You won't be the only one
Celebrating with this cry:
"It's exploded!" – my, oh my!

As I've just said, this strategy was quite evident at FART, although, strictly speaking, we weren't a part of the private sector: we were a so-called quango – a semi-public administrative body outside the civil service but receiving financial support from the government. But, whatever you are, you will surely be keen to adopt a good idea when you see one. So we had these endless meetings. And the more meetings you attended, the more impressive your annual self-appraisal was perceived to be. The back-to-back ones were the best. Unfortunately, this in itself didn't appear to be sufficient for us to get all the money we would have liked. We were thus a bit peeved when we noticed that the government was using lots of our dosh to bribe the industry, although they called all this money essential subsidies.

In principle, I have nothing against essential subsidies: I've just told you that we could have done with extra dough. However, none came to us. Why? We were developing national qualifications, after all. But then somebody explained that, while a car manufacturer or steel producer could easily relocate to another country – quite possibly in Europe (imagine the sheer horror of this!) – we couldn't. Unless we wanted to switch to developing Danish qualifications, but this would be a tad impractical because none of us spoke Danish. Or had any idea about the Danish education system. Not that some of our bosses had much idea about our own education system either: when a navy commander retires, you have to find him a plum job in Civvy Street, don't you? So you put him in charge of developing national qualifications, although he hasn't got a clue.

Apropos bribing, I mean subsiding, the industry, our current government is planning to bung £500 million of taxpayers' money to Tata Steel. And what does Tata Steel do? It announces a shutdown of blast furnaces at Port Talbot, which would put thousands of jobs in South Wales at risk. That's gratitude for you.

Returning to all this promised change, one thing in Rishi Sunak's conference speech really caught my eye – or, rather, ear – namely his proposal to bundle A- and T-levels into a new advanced qualification requiring students to study maths and English to eighteen alongside three other subjects. That's what the rest of the world is doing, so it's not exactly revolutionary, but quite a change for England and Wales. Scotland and Northern Ireland have their own education systems, of course. Actually, I can see his point. My commentary on the teaching of English – particularly the principles organising written English – would fill several books, a few of which I have already written, so let me make an observation about maths. But, first, I have another confession to make: I can't resist a special offer. We writers aren't made of money, you know. Not with my books being priced at less than ten quid, and with the current price of *Writers' and Artists' Yearbook* being £30. *£30!* In the mists of time, when I started writing books in English, it was only £10! Besides, we hadn't had any special offers under communism: everything was in such short supply that our nationalised commerce knew it would be able to flog whatever our nationalised industry had knocked up. So seeing all those special deals in Britain was a complete revelation, and, although I pride myself on being able to resist all sorts of external pressures, I'm a sucker for cut-price offers. Such as this: one of our local supermarkets has recently introduced this amazing multi-buy deal – *two* jars of olives for £5. So far so good: they are large jars. But an individual jar costs £2.49! This is probably why England and Wales need to extend the compulsory teaching of maths until the age of eighteen. In the meantime, I can have fun with ditties such as this one.

Given my depleted coffers,
I am keen on special offers,
So I set off with a flounce,
And, on seeing *Sale*, I pounce.

As for *Buy One Get One Free*,
I cannot conceal my glee,
Rushing in and grabbing stuff,
With no switch that says 'enough'.

What is more, when I am low,
Seeing *Everything Must Go*
Absolutely makes my day:
There'll be bargains there – oh, yay!

And, however hard I try,
The allure of *Multi-Buy*
Is too tempting to resist:
Deals are never to be missed.

So you can imagine how
Thrilled I am that now, *right now*,
Our local superstore
Advertises deals galore,

Such as olives (those in brine)
At two pounds and forty-nine;
Buying two* would cost five quid;
That's *exactly* what I did!

**Jars – not olives*

So I am fully with Rishi on this one.

Anna (always sporting a visor) with Liz, her friend and fellow Roamer, atop the freezing Great Calva, 2022

Anna with her lovely Skiddaw u3a Roamers atop Blea Rigg, 2024

Anna with her lovely Skiddaw u3a Roamers atop Kentmere Pike, 2022

Anna with Paul, a friend and fellow Roamer, atop Sheffield Pike, 2022

Anna with her lovely Skiddaw u3a Roamers atop Catbells, 2022

Anna with her lovely Skiddaw u3a Roamers on Kentmere Pike again, 2023

Anna against a spectacular rainbow on Hartsop above How, 2023

Anna with her lovely Skiddaw u3a Roamers on Yewbarrow, 2023

Anna with her lovely Skiddaw u3a Roamers on Gowbarrow, 2023

Anna with Robin, a friend, fellow Roamer and our IT supremo, atop Catstycam, 2023

Anna with her lovely Skiddaw u3a
Roamers on Lank Rigg, 2023

Anna with her lovely Skiddaw u3a
Roamers atop Souther Fell, 2023

Anna with her lovely Skiddaw u3a Roamers on Scathwaite Fell, 2023

Anna with Bobby, not a Roamer but a special friend nevertheless, on High Spy, 2024

Anna with Moira, a friend and fellow Roamer, atop High Rigg, 2024

Anna with her lovely Skiddaw u3a Roamers on Walla Crag, 2024

12

Stagecoach and Me, My Guardian Angel, Adders on Shap ~~Fells~~, the Other Borrowdale and the Claife Heights Mishap

Since one of my missions (it's not only politicians who can have missions, you know, although theirs often come to naught) is to illustrate what can be achieved by using public transport – someone has to, after all – I will continue in this vein here. I hope our bus provider, Stagecoach, will take note of my efforts. In the summer of 2023, they treated us to some extra-smart new buses, and I really think they should educate the public on how to use them – particularly the tourists. For example, they could recommend bringing earplugs for the ride. On the super-popular 555 route, they make announcements before every stop, which is extremely helpful, but each announcement is preceded by a loud jingle, which invariably makes you jump. They have also installed nice tables on the top deck, but this means that more seats face each other. And I've already told you what happens then. So they should definitely advise folk that putting their feet on seats is very poor form. And they may also wish to point out that their lovely drivers are not tourist information officers. I mean, they are very helpful anyway, and I am all for their being able to answer all bus-stop-related questions. Or to tell a tourist who wants to go to Kendal that this bus actually goes in the opposite direction – namely to Keswick. Or to advise them on the asked-for connection, which won't involve more than a two-hour wait. But when a visitor boards the bus, pulls out his or her map, opens it and then tries to engage the driver in a conversation about the route of their planned walk, the resulting five-minute hold-up is not ideal. Things like that. So I reckon that Stagecoach ought to produce their very own leaflet on how to use their buses. And when they do, they should now know whom to contract for the job. My rates are quite reasonable.

Despite the best efforts of bus and train companies, however, public transport users in the Lake District will also require a dollop of luck thrown in for good measure. Okay, and the odd taxi for when their luck runs out. In Book 1, I recounted lots of my hikes made possible by public transport, but, by now, you will undoubtedly have become aware of my strategy. What do you mean *what strategy*? Not the pre-election one, obviously, but one of holding stuff back for my next book. And now I'm reaping the rewards because I haven't yet told you about this adventure.

Eleven summers ago, they laid on this fantastic shuttle minibus running from Seascale to Wasdale Head and linking with the equally fabulous morning train running along the Cumbrian Coast. Just the ticket for the likes of me. Quite a few tickets, actually. Despite my essentially solitary nature, I had, by then, acquired a few adventurous friends, Patti and Julian among them, and they agreed to go along with my scheme. We caught an early bus to Workington, where we changed for the coastal train, disembarking at Seascale. There, the pre-booked minibus was waiting for us, depositing us at Greendale at the foot of Wasdale's Middle Fell. From the hamlet, apparently the residence of the legendary fell runner Joss Naylor, we slogged our way up Seatallan across its vast marshy slope rising above Greendale Gill. Whatever possessed A. Wainwright to include this route in his guide? All was well in the gill's ravine, but Nether Wasdale Common, which may be nether but is also elevated and wet, has nothing to commend it. Actually, maybe that's why it's common: nobody wants to appropriate it purely for themselves.

No matter. Having enjoyed the view from the summit of Seatallan, we plodded across the undulating plateau to Haycock, whose rocky summit was attained after the steep bypass of Gowder Crag. The usual descent along the main Ennerdale ridge then conveyed us to the sprawling top of Caw Fell, beyond which our adventure began. I had been desperate to try out Caw Fell's south-west shoulder descending to Blengdale Forest. Why? Because no one ventures there. At least, no one from Keswick. Isn't that a good enough reason? Regrettably, our pathless descent along the shoulder wasn't nearly as appealing as it looked on the map.

> Oh, how these ridges mystify!
> Some will be low, some will be high;
> You want to explore,
> But this one's a bore;
> There is no path? You can see why.

Eventually, after a long hard slog – cross-country tramping is likely to be better for your quadriceps than for your morale – we reached the edge of Blengdale Forest, which I had visited previously and found delightful. No, not the edge itself but the whole forest. The wide tracks intersecting it did not disappoint, and we made good progress – until we reached the River Bleng. Oops, where is the bridge? At the bottom of the river was the answer. What do we do now? Like caged animals, we paced there and back along the riverbank but could see no passage we might be able to make use of. We were, however, on a tight schedule: a taxi pre-booked by me (no, not Garry's: we were too far away from Keswick) was supposed to pick us up from Wellington Bridge (just outside Gosforth) in little more than half an hour. So we had to invoke our respective guardian angels, gird up our loins and wade across the river. Scary. Apropos my own guardian angel, she seemed to have been getting progressively more and more bad-tempered. Can't think why.

> My guardian angel seemed very cross:
> Listen to me, I am your boss,
> What do you think you're playing at
> Testing me so, you daft old bat?

I nearly did a double-take
Seeing you scrambling up Jack's Rake,
And, on Sharp Edge, you will recall,
I very nearly let you fall.

The Grasmoor route? I rolled my eyes:
Climbing straight up was not that wise;
Up this steep chimney, I saw your dread
But did decide: let her go red;

Why did you think, by Piers Gill,
That this rough route would be a thrill?
On Catstycam's steep North-west Ridge,
You felt some fear – more than a smidge;

Bowfell's traverse was not that hard,
But it was icy and left you scarred;
Just as I started my downtime,
You fancied yet another climb:

Up Pillar straight from Ennerdale –
I felt I couldn't make you fail;
As for your trespass on The Nab,
Where was your talent of the gab?

I had to laugh, but I am irked:
You keep me very overworked;
Fisher's Wife's Rake? Covered in screes:
You had to use your hands and knees;

> Yewbarrow's scrambles made you freeze;
> Why did you think they'd be a breeze?
> And Mellbreak set a nasty trap:
> This Pillar Rake did make you flap.
>
> You really think that it's just you?
> I have got other crazies too:
> Just stop these exploits and behave,
> Making this one your last close shave!

Somehow, I have a strong suspicion that I wasn't my guardian angel's favourite charge. Anyway, we managed to wade across the river. Luckily, the bridleway on the other side was comfortable, which is just as well because, at this point in the proceedings, we had no option but to run. Having reached Wellington Bridge, we collapsed on the bench, completely out of puff. And the taxi arrived just a moment later! Despite my lifelong experience of timing myself, I will never know how, after such a long hike, I managed to get us to the finishing line to within a minute. Patti and Julian were dumbfounded. After the taxi delivered us back to Seascale, the further logistics were merely a case of repeating the morning operation in reverse. Unfortunately, the summer of the Wasdale shuttle was extremely wet, and the service didn't seem to attract enough punters. So they pulled it: just like the X33 and some other ephemeral summer buses I told you about in Book 1. And the one below, but I haven't recounted this particular story yet.

Imagine being able to explore the remote Shap Fells by using buses – unbelieve! But you could. First of all, though, you had to get yourself to Penrith on a very early bus. Then you would change for the two-hourly service to Kendal. The bus you wanted would leave Penrith at 9am, and you would have a lovely ride along the A6 all the way to Shap. Unfortunately, past Shap the bus would abandon the A6, moving away from the fells, so you had to ask the lovely driver to let you off between bus stops because you needed to get as close to Wet Sleddale Reservoir as possible. After all, you were faced with more than fifteen miles of tramping, some of it cross-country, and you didn't want to add even one unnecessary inch. The lovely driver would invariably oblige, and you would dart down the minor road towards the reservoir. I had, by then, acquired the eighth guidebook by A. Wainright – that covering the Outlying Fells of Lakeland – and, having scaled all the main ones several times over, I made it my mission to conquer all of the outlying ones.

So I had studied said guidebook before embarking on this particular adventure, which starts once you have cleared the reservoir. But A. Wainwright tells you fibs: where is this blinking trail, which looks so enticing on the page? So easy just to draw a line – so hard to find the actual path. One thing he was truthful about: rough walking in heather. You climb up this wet, rivulet-intersected, slope towards Sleddale Pike, trying not to sink too deep into the holes concealed by the scratchy heather carpeting the entire sprawling hillside. Then you have to tramp across the desolate, pathless, moorland to reach Wasdale Pike. Finally, a respite: from the top of your pike, you can see a track following the wide ridge, so you stick with it like glue, soon emerging on the summit of Great Yarlside.

From there, the route following the wall to Harrop Pike is actually quite pleasant: you are travelling across a vast, largely grassy, expanse of rounded fells forming several horseshoes and delight in the peacefulness of the area and in your solitude. You are, though, somewhat discombobulated by the rather unexpected notice warning you about adders, which, apparently, reside in this area. Have you got anything on you that could be used as a tourniquet? A belt, maybe? It is your understanding that, after you get bitten by an adder, you have to stop the flow of blood from the site of the bite. But what if you recline on a stone, and an adder bites you on the neck? You must never, *ever* recline on a stone. Or even sit on one. Or sit down *anywhere*. You thus eat your lunch standing up: you haven't met any humans since the beginning of your heathery climb (can't think why), so there would be nobody to help you. And even though the notice gives the phone number to call in an emergency, how long before your rescuers could reach you?

You try hard to banish those pesky thoughts from your mind, an attempt which, past Harrop Pike, is gratifyingly successful because you have to use all your powers of concentration to navigate the bog separating the top from the summit of Grey Crag. And you don't think adders live in bogs. Although Grey Crag is quite remote, you have already climbed it several times (ways and means), so you know which way to descend to Sadgill in Longsleddale. Further down, the route is quite steep, yes, but at least you know where you stand. In the main: the bottom section of the slope is covered in shoulder-height bracken, so it's not always possible to see where you actually stand. Anyway, you are now right at the bottom of the long valley, but, in order to get yourself closer to civilisation, you now have to climb out of it. Thankfully, a track ascending in the direction of the still-distant Kentmere provides the solution, and you soon branch off onto a bridleway heading towards the even more distant Staveley. But, unlike Kentmere, Staveley has a bus stop! You dash – there is now no option of proceeding at a more dignified pace – across Green Quarter Fell and Staveley Head Fell until you reach the tarmacked Hall Lane, where you can pick up even more speed. Finally, you get to your bus stop in Staveley to the applause of the passers-by: your velocity is, indeed, impressive. Phew, you have made the last bus, but only just. If you should miss it, however, it's a Garry job, I'm afraid. It will cost you a few quid, but it's your own stupid fault for abandoning your driving lessons after a mere year and a half of intensive instruction. Mind you, your traumatised driving instructor is still in recovery – even after all those years.

I have had many more adventures on Shap Fells, but I must leave some stuff for later: you never know, my publisher might even ask me to write another book. Not that I have any immediate plans to continue in a similar vein in my next opus, which, for a change, will satirise jargon and bureaucracy. I may, however, decide to return to this format at some stage in the future: the ammunition is there. But I mustn't get ahead of myself.

This marvellous Penrith-to-Kendal bus could transport an unmotorised Keswickian such as me as far as 'the other Borrowdale' in Westmorland and even to the fabulous Howgills (between the Lake District and the Yorkshire Dales). Said Keswickian could then return home to her bed on the same day – unbelievable! And most welcome: this particular Keswickian can't abide sleeping in strange beds. This would be impossible now. No, not sleeping in strange beds – although that is also nigh on impossible, what with said Keswickian's deep dislike of travel – but using this bus. Because they pulled it. But, who knows, they may reinstate it one day. Maybe when we get all this growth going and the economy improves. *If* we get all this growth going and the economy improves.

Anyway, to reach 'the other Borrowdale', you'd need to go all the way to Low Borrow Bridge, elegantly spanning Borrow Beck in the spectacular Lune Gorge. You would travel there via Shap, Orton and Tebay, enjoying lovely scenery. You would then hop off the bus and follow the beck into the valley, where you would have several options. By far the best would be to tackle the entire horseshoe taking in all the fells fringing the valley, the Whinfell Ridge on its southern flank being magnificent. Completely hooked, I kept returning to explore the area, varying the route each time I went. Then – a disaster: I learnt that they were going to kill the bus! On that fateful day, the weather forecast was rather grim, but I didn't care: although I now knew 'the other Borrowdale' quite well, the only fell in the vicinity I hadn't yet climbed was Grayrigg Common, with Grayrigg Pike thereon, and this was my very last opportunity to bag it.

So off I went, fully waterproofed and fortified by a devil-may-care attitude. It was already drizzling when I started my ascent up the wooded hillside towards the rim above the deep hollow of Little and Great Coums. There was still some visibility, and I tried not to succumb to vertigo as I looked down the precipice. From the guide by A. Wainwright, I knew that there would be an Ordnance Survey column on the summit of Grayrigg Common, so I was hugely relieved when I finally reached it. Alas, the very extensive panorama advertised by the author was non-existent: I was now in a thick soup and could see nothing. So, again, I had to invoke my guardian angel – actually, she'd had a point – and commenced my descent blind.

The map was no use – it was too windy and rainy – which means that I wouldn't have been able to use a compass anyway. That is, if I had learnt how to use it in the first place. I'm slipping on wet grass and stumbling over slippery stones, desperately trying to remember the contours on the map. Suddenly, why am I in a gully? I was meant to be going down a slope rather than getting stuck in gullies. So I scramble back up and am now guided purely by the gradient, which isn't supposed to be severe. I stagger down, eventually locating a trail, which I then follow. Finally, I'm beginning to be able to discern some contours further away. Slowly, my field of vision widens, and I can see that I am descending into a valley. But it's far too open to be Borrowdale – where exactly am I? Well, wherever I am, I can now discern some sort of dwelling, so civilisation can't be too far away. The lumpy terrain is marshy, but, eventually, I come across a path, which winds its way down to a small village. Grayrigg! Not at all where I had been planning to end up – but on a bus route: my guardian angel had come up trumps yet again! And the bus servicing this route was the same I had been on in the morning, although I would now travel in the opposite direction, changing buses in Kendal rather than Penrith.

While the service was running, I was even able to explore the beguiling Howgills, which I adore nearly as much as I do the Lakes, but my reminiscences thereof will have to await their turn. Before I bring this chapter to a close, I would like to recount one more escapade made possible by public transport. The logistics are as follows: you bus it from Keswick to Windermere, where you change for the bus to the madly busy Bowness, where you dash to the Windermere ferry terminal, where you board the ferry, whereon you cross the lake before disembarking on its west side, where you enjoy a magnificent walk around the peaceful Claife Heights area before catching your return bus in Hawkshead and returning thereon to Ambleside, where you change for the Keswick bus. Easy-peasy: second nature to me.

I thought my dear friend Bobby might enjoy this escapade, which was also to be my recce for the walk I was going to take my lovely Roamers on. After all, Claife Heights is a delightful, largely afforested, upland rising between Lake Windermere and Esthwaite. The weather was beautiful, we were both in high spirits, and all went well until we reached the western shore of Windermere. Even there, we had no inkling of what lay in store for us. We greatly enjoyed visiting the popular Claife viewing station, offering fabulous views of Lake Windermere. Formerly a Gothic tower, it was built during the Picturesque movement and is now being maintained by the National Trust. From there, we followed a lovely, if steepish, path ascending across the wooded slope below Mitchell Knotts before reaching a wide track undulating its way north towards the highest part of the upland, High

Blind How. I knew the area well and was delighted to be able to introduce Bobby to its charms.

On we stroll, but, suddenly, what's this? A tape blocking our route. Why? I look around and spot a sign announcing that the passage ahead is blocked because of forest operations. But we need to get ourselves to the bus in Hawkshead! How bad can it get? I've overcome much worse obstacles, surely. Today is Saturday, so they won't be working, and we should be okay. We thus simply step over the tape and keep going. But, soon, we understand: the trees previously covering the entire area have been felled and are now reduced to jagged tree stumps, with fallen branches, surely more than a foot deep, completely obliterating the path. What's even worse, the heavy machinery has churned up the ground quite badly, so your choice is as follows: either sink up to your ankles in the mud or get trapped by the tangle of branches, where you go in even deeper. Imagine my mortification: I had promised Bobby a lovely walk!

It took us ages to extricate ourselves, at which point we no longer had enough time for a leisurely return to Hawkshead. But we did make our bus, and Bobby, inexplicably, remains my good friend to this day. You have to admire his adventurous spirit!

13

My Birketts Obsession, My Lovely Roamers, Sleep Trackers and Other Gizmos and My Potassium Level

Much as I love solitude, I also adore walking with my delightful Roamers. In Book 1, I recounted some mishaps which had occurred on our walks, but there have been more. The Lakeland challenges I had set myself included not only scaling the 214 Wainwright mountains *at least* ten times each (many will have been climbed dozens of times, with a few favourites visited on hundreds of occasions) and climbing all the outlying fells but also bagging the so-called Birketts: 541 Lake District fells over 1,000 feet high. With the first two goals already accomplished, you can't blame me for wanting to make it a hat trick, can you? By the way, when I first came to this wonderful country, I thought that this phrase meant a trick you performed with a hat. But I have since been educated. So, whenever I get the opportunity, I try to add a Birkett or two to my collection. Such as when we climbed Pike o' Blisco from Great Langdale. The magnificent route ascended across the craggy slope of Wrynose Fell.

Apropos Wrynose, the fell had lent its name to a well-known pass – Wrynose Pass – and our tourist information centres receive a lot of questions from visitors about it – understandably. One of such enquiries rather took the adviser by surprise because it referred to Rhinoceros Pass. Wrynose is pronounced in the same way as 'rhinos', so the tourist had put two and two together and… come up with Rhinoceros Pass. At least the information officer had a good laugh. Back en route to Pike o' Blisco, we stopped for elevenses at the foot of Long Crag. And what is Long Crag? A Birkett! Too good an opportunity to pass up. So I told my charges to take their time over coffee and darted off. Behind Long Crag is Blake Rigg – another Birkett! Although I ran as fast as I could, it still took half an hour to bag both Birketts, so my group had a long coffee break. They were very understanding, but I vowed never to pull a stunt like this *ever again* – and have never done. I got this verse out of it, though.

> She's notorious on the circuit:
> "Not another flaming Birkett!"
> They exclaim in sheer despair
> As they catch her hungry stare.
>
> She has only gone and found
> Yet another hidden mound
> Dwarfed by finer-looking fells,
> And she's off – she *is* – hell's bells!

> That's the last thing that they need:
> She does have a group to lead;
> Are they, in this rough terrain,
> To be stranded *yet again*?
>
> But there's nothing to be done:
> To her, Birketts are great fun
> And a challenge (just like bait),
> So they have to sit and wait.
>
> But they know it is her passion,
> So they've brought an extra ration;
> Next time, though (and that's well meant),
> They had better bring a tent!

Well, my lovely Roamers hadn't been left stranded *again*, but I needed a rhyme for 'terrain'. You don't, however, need to get stranded to have your endurance tested: the Lake District mountains may not be very high, but they can spring all sorts of surprises on you. October is a good time to observe the red deer rut in full swing – if you know where to look. And I certainly did. Actually, if you check online, you will find quite a few ads enticing you to part with good money in exchange for being guided to deer rutting places. That's what I mean by the western knack for monetising things, which I have never acquired. Consequently, my lovely Roamers get treated to this spectacle for free. We travelled to Burnbanks, at the foot of Haweswater. Using a section of the iconic Coast to Coast route running along the reservoir, we soon reached the cascading Measand Beck and followed it upstream before tackling the steep ascent up Measand End. By the time we reached the rim of the deep basin of Whelter Bottom below Low Raise, we'd seen many red deer and heard a lot of bellows, but now the orchestra of roars intensified, their sound reverberating loudly across the entire area. And when we looked down into the basin, we could see its steep slopes literally covered in red deer, the hinds busily grazing and stags charging back and forth in an impressive display of their prowess and occasionally engaging in head-on combat.

It was hard to break the spell, but time was pressing, so we continued to Low Raise before descending along the fell's interesting, albeit pathless, south-east ridge. And right at the bottom sat the innocuous looking Castle Crag – a Birkett. While climbing it was easy and did not require a detour, it was the descent to the main Haweswater path that was truly crucifying. In his guide, Bill Birkett advises that 'descent is probably best made to the north, where an ancient track becomes submerged in bracken'. And submerged it certainly was – and not only in bracken. The long tussocky grass (the longest I'd ever encountered) concealed deep holes, and, as we staggered, we kept slipping and falling into them. To make matters worse, some of them were filled with water, so the passage was most unpleasant. Thankfully, the terrain wasn't steep, and this section was relatively short, but Castle Crag attained the dubious distinction of becoming my joint worst Birkett – alongside Great Bank on the side of Irton Fell in Eskdale. And did anyone complain? Not my lovely Roamers! In fact, they all said how much they had enjoyed this adventurous hike and, throughout the following year, kept asking me if I was going to repeat it in the coming October. This I duly did, although we gave Castle Crag a wide berth. *Very* wide.

On returning from another Birkett, Carron Crag in Grizedale Forest, my group actually managed to lose *me*! Grizedale Forest is criss-crossed by amazing trails, and I love the area with a passion. Because I can get to it by using a combination of two buses (each way), I had explored it thoroughly and had led quite a few walks around the area – both for my lovely Roamers and for Keswick Rambling Club, which is equally lovely. But, on that occasion, I was recovering from a hip replacement operation (I told you all about it you know where) so wasn't the fastest – not that I am particularly fast anyway (unless I'm sprinting to catch a bus, that is). What is the point of charging ahead and missing the delightful sights all around you? As we followed the forest road leading towards High Cross, where we had parked our cars, there formed an advance group, which got further and further away from the rest of us. Suddenly, we lost sight of it completely. But in it was a dear friend of mine, one of my stalwarts, who was an experienced walker. Besides, she carried with her a gizmo apparently telling her which way to go, so I wasn't worried. Having an analogue mindset, I myself possessed no such gadgets – I still don't. Some of you will have read all about my technological ineptitude: Book 1 did sell three copies, you know, and they might even have been passed around. Then again, you can go wrong even with a thingy supposedly telling you where to go. Another friend of mine, new to the area, was using one to guide her to the summit of Ullscarf but ended up on top of

Seat Sandal, which sits on the opposite side of the valley. That's 180 degrees out. My only concession to modernity was my reluctant acquisition of a mobile phone. No, not a smartphone or an iPhone: just a Doro – a granny phone. What's wrong with a granny phone anyway? It does make phone calls. And, amazingly, receives them. Isn't this what a phone is supposed to do? Admittedly, you need to have it switched on, which I hardly ever do, carrying it with me for emergencies only. But I have no children to keep tabs on and couldn't keep tabs on Vinnie if I tried: he possesses no mobile phone at all.

Anyway, there we were, unconcerned about the walkers in the advance group armed with their amazing gizmo: their drivers were with them, and our driver was among us. On reaching the car park, my little group of four laggards got into our car and merrily drove home. I don't pay any attention to cars, by the way: ask me what vehicles my friends are driving, and I won't be able to tell you. The best I can come up with is the car's colour. But only of two cars anyway: Jacqui's is red and Clive's is black (did I remember correctly, Clive?). So, in the car park, I assumed that the fast Roamers had already gone. What subsequently transpired, however, was that the advance party had gone wrong at one of the junctions, following a more obvious, but wrong, route. I, on the other hand, knew exactly which way to go, so reaching the car park was entirely unproblematic – with no need for gadgets of any description to show us the way. Meanwhile, the advance group must have realised that they had gone wrong and waited for us. And waited. *And waited* (as usual, my granny phone was switched off: we didn't need Mountain Rescue, after all, did we?). But, in the dense forest, they couldn't see us, apart from which we simply weren't following the same track. After more than half an hour, they gave up and somehow managed to get themselves back to High Cross, returning home much later than us. Serves them right for abandoning the leader! We had many more adventures, of course, but this seems an appropriate moment for a few more philosophical reflections on modern technology.

As we rambled far and wide, I noticed something deeply concerning. One of my lovely Roamers was getting more and more withdrawn, with unexpected bursts of irritability. He developed puffy eyes, his hands started shaking and the dark circles under his eyes were more pronounced every time I saw him. Even more worryingly, he started stumbling on our walks, an affliction which, at height, can be very dangerous. That's when I realised that I needed to get to the bottom of things. And the bottom of things is not easy to reach, I can tell you. Plus, he was a man. You know how it is with men. You don't? Men find it much harder to open up than women. Otherwise, they are fine. Actually, there is a long verse about men in Book 1, so some of you will be aware of my general approval. But, with my wilting walking companion, who was relatively new to the group, I knew I would need a subtle strategy. You don't think I can do subtle? But this book is full of subtleties…

Anyway, my strategy was to engage him in an innocent conversation about his hobbies. It transpired that he was very interested in all sorts of gadgets. Any new electronic gizmo on the market, and he would be the first in the queue. So what had he been buying? He perked up a bit and gave me a long list. Some of it was double Dutch to me, but what I did understand was that he was very keen on measuring and analysing all sorts of his bodily functions: blood pressure, heart rate, cholesterol levels, kidney function, liver function, thyroid function, metabolism, respiration, digestion, excretion, things like that. But he was particularly interested in what running was doing to his body: he was a long-distance runner, you see. Not a runner-for-the-bus such as me – a *proper* runner. He specifically mentioned Libre Freestyle 2 Continuous Glucose Monitor for checking his glucose levels. He also said something about carrying out biomechanical evaluation with the help from RunScribe. Apparently, you had a pod on each foot and one on your waistband – who would have thought? He also mentioned Strava, Minetti, Garmin, GitHub and Stryd, adding triumphantly that he had just got himself a next gen Stryd – yippee! And did you know that you could even use an iPhone as a running sensor? Mind-blowing.

My ears pricked up when he confessed, with slight annoyance, that he was so absorbed in tinkering (for goodness' sake, don't tell him I called his passion tinkering) with his latest thirty-eight gadgets that he had neglected to replace his old sleep tracker, which had given up the ghost. Thankfully, some six weeks previously, he had rectified his omission. Some six weeks previously? But that's exactly when I started noticing his worrying symptoms! Could it have been…? It *must* have been his sleep tracker! The poor man *must* have been obsessing about his sleep to such an extent that his anxiety was preventing him from sleeping – bingo!

You are always very tired?
Then I know what is required:
There's a gizmo – I'm a backer –
That will help you: a sleep tracker.

They have now become quite cheap
And will help you with your sleep.
It may be a thing you wear –
There are many to compare:

If it's hidden in a watch,
Then it's bound to be top-notch;
One concealed within a ring?
It could also be the thing.

If you get yourself a strap,
It will analyse each nap
Alongside each nightly slumber;
What a clever little number!

And you'll find a mattress topper
To be also good and proper,
Whereas a sleep-tracing mat
Also works, though it is flat.

You are keen to test their worth
In your bed or on your berth,
So you check and stress and fret
About sleep that you do get.

> Your anxiety is such
> That you cannot sleep that much
> And are now completely spent;
> Yep, I get your discontent
>
> But technology is brill,
> So don't worry and just chill:
> There's a gizmo – I'm a backer –
> That will cancel your sleep tracker!

When, however, I tried to share my theory with him – subtly, of course – he became indignant and stopped coming on my walks. So maybe I need to work on my subtlety, after all... Be that as it may, my introduction to the wonders of modern technology continues. After years of determined resistance, I caved in and am now on Facebook. Don't worry, there are no personal details there; my date of birth is fake, 'contact and basic info' is left blank, and I wouldn't disclose my 'life events' there if you paid me big bucks. Besides, I have my books to do this for me. I also don't announce to all and sundry when I'm going on holiday, adding, for the sake of absolute clarity, that my house will be left empty for the following five weeks. All I do on Facebook is post my walking pictures there. But friends' posts are an education. Until recently, for example, I had thought that HR stood for Human Resources. When, however, this particular Roamer, the runner, whom I continue to follow on Facebook (he hadn't blocked me), referred to 'tweaking his max HR', I started having doubts. It transpires that this acronym stands for heart rate. What's more, apparently you can correlate your maximal oxygen intake with your maximum heart rate – did you know that? And you can also check your overnight heart rate response. Well, as long as you don't lose any sleep over it. Personally, I'm just happy to have a heart rate at all. And having a pulse is also a definite plus; I don't need a tracker to determine that it's still there.

I have a salutary tale for you here. I, too, had once wanted to know how my body was performing so asked my GP practice for the results of my most recent blood and urine tests. What's the harm in asking Dr Google for a second opinion, after all? So I pored over all the data, trying to figure out what was what. All was well until I got to the level of potassium in my urine (not blood, thankfully): it was sky-high – absolutely off the scale. Whereupon I had an absolute meltdown: I tidied my knicker drawer (although, with no knicker shops in Keswick, it was nearly empty), booked an urgent appointment with my solicitor to update my will and gave Vinnie detailed instructions vis-à-vis my funeral: low-key with no fuss, no mourning and no eulogy, bright clothing for the attendees (all three of them) and the song *Great Balls of Fire* to accompany my eco-friendly coffin's slide into the furnace. After a period of reflection, however, I realised that my potassium levels were off the charts simply because I live on fruit, vegetables, nuts and seeds – all rich in potassium. And fish. No western, potassium-depleted, diet for me. So I'm fine now, my potassium level notwithstanding.

Returning to Facebook, when a post of this particular Facebook friend mentioned TSB, I nearly asked him about his personal experience with Trustee Savings Bank. But I didn't – because we had fallen out. It subsequently transpired, however, that the acronym stood for Training Stress Balance, which you can also measure. Isn't this simply marvellous? And take TRIMP. I thought a trimp was a woman who was both weak and shy but also flirtatious. It transpires it's Training Impulse, and the excellent thing about Training Impulse is that it can be modelled – wow! In another of his posts, he made the following confession: 'I enjoy HIIT but prefer LSD'. While I was not at all surprised, I thought it was rather brave of him to admit to dabbling in drugs, even though many of our politicians had made a similar confession. I think anybody would prefer a psychedelic trip after all this High Intensity Interval Training, which, apparently, is what HIIT stands for. They say that oral digestion of LSD is the safest. But then the post said something about Garmin data and Stryd data, so I started having doubts about this LSD – maybe he didn't mean a narcotic, after all? Whatever it is (the post didn't decode this acronym), I imagine it can also be measured, pored over and plotted on a graph... fantastic! To a technological dinosaur such as me, the only appropriate acronym to use at this juncture is OMG! And don't forget about my potassium-level tale when you take and analyse all these measurements.

I've already told you that I am an expert map reader. Well, most of the time. And this young IT whizz points at my map and laughs. And, when he finishes laughing, he remarks, still chortling: "A *paper* map! How quaint!" *Quaint?* Young man, this paper map has guided me to tens of thousands of mountain peaks and along tens of thousands of miles of mountainous terrain. Maybe not *this* particular one, but you get my drift. And my paper map never runs out of battery power or needs a digital signal to work either. It was my turn to laugh when another young friend of mine was panicking: apparently, his diary had crashed, and he had lost contact details of all his friends. The only crashing *my* leather-bound diary does is when it falls from the shelf onto the floor, but, even then, it doesn't lose any information. Technology has its limitations – even the GPSs used by some of my lovely Roamers on our walks. Whenever we compare all the data at the end, no two readings are the same, with both the mileage and the amount of ascent varying quite considerably between the different gizmos. I, on the other hand, estimate the mileage to be covered by placing a piece of string on the map – and the result is usually more accurate than theirs!

> GPSs and smartphones they bring,
> "This is it," they all say, "that's the thing!"
> Of this there's no doubt:
> Their mileage is out,
> But she does get it right with her string…

Anyway, enough about gizmos.

14

The Context, Delightful Creatures, Mum's Cattery Incident, the Missing Comma and More on My Lovely Roamers

They say that we are led by donkeys. How lovely: I like donkeys. So I can't understand why they don't seem too happy when they are saying this. They also say that Britain doesn't need any more rabbits. I know I've already told you this, but what I haven't mentioned is the context. And context is extremely important. That's what all the politicians invoke when they have been cornered and are having to explain themselves.

> Context is what will explain
> Actions causing people pain,
> Daft decisions, crazy schemes,
> Rules that rob you of your dreams.

> You will see, 'cos you're not dense,
> All of them make perfect sense
> Put in context; in that light,
> It is clear that we were right!

Take Dr Death's, sorry, Rishi Sunak's, decision to launch his 'Eat Out to Help Out' scheme in the middle of the Covid pandemic. They said it was hare-brained: so unfair on the poor hares. I think they should get together with rabbits to form a united front in order to fight against such blatant prejudice. Of course, at the Covid inquiry the now prime minister invoked the context, this being a surefire way to redemption.

Returning to the persecuted rabbits, it was actually *The Economist* that objected to their being pulled out of hats. Very disappointing to an animal lover such as myself. But I've promised you the context: this otherwise august magazine was referring to the national insurance cut unexpectedly announced by Jeremy Hunt, the chancellor, in his 2023 Autumn Statement. It was, of course, the same national insurance whose rates *absolutely* needed to be increased in order to fund social care. As recently as January 2022, both Johnson and Sunak were adamant that the rise was 'the right plan' which 'must go ahead'. Consequently, the Conservative MPs approved it. And now, less than two years later, 'the right plan' suddenly became the wrong plan – and the Conservative MPs, again, concurred. That's why *The Economist* has likened them to sheep, meekly following the government even when it veers all over the place with no clear sense of direction. Some more animal discrimination: poor sheep!

Clearly, the magazine hasn't seen our Lakeland sheep in action: meekly following is simply not on their agenda. Those hard-working sheep dogs have their work cut out, I can tell you.

Politics aside, I think we should be more appreciative of both our wildlife and our domestic animals. Given that I am a *genuine* animal lover, I have thus decided to devote this chapter to animal encounters. Well, a part of it, because that's also where I'm going to tell you a bit more about my lovely Roamers. Strictly speaking, I wouldn't need to if I could be *certain* that you've read Book 1, but, sadly, I'm harbouring deep suspicions. But let's start with animals.

> Here is a froglet called Croak,
> So nice in his shiny green cloak;
> He lives in our pond,
> Of flies he is fond;
> Don't give him a prod or a poke.

Aw, isn't that sweet? I can do sweet, you know. If I put my mind to it. Or this.

> Desmond is a handsome duck,
> But he goes cluck, cluck, cluck, cluck:
> He's a little thick,
> Thinking he's a chick,
> With the hens, though, he hasn't much luck.

You also like dogs, don't you? So do I.

> This doggie does have quite a bark,
> Loves chasing a ball round the park,
> Then, quite out of breath,
> Will lick you to death
> And poop right in front – what a lark!

I was once walking in one of our beautiful Keswick parks and saw what must have been the smallest dog to have ever graced this Earth. It was so tiny that if would have fitted in the palm of your hand. Then his owner turns around and beckons his pet by calling his name – Wellington! Such a majestic name for such a miniscule creature. If incongruity ever needed to be illustrated, I can't think of a better example. This amusing encounter has inspired the limerick below.

> There once was this doggie called Killer,
> So christened by one Mr Miller;
> While lively and cute,
> He was quite minute
> And no use if you wanted a thriller.

I'm less sure about mice, though. The field ones are perfectly sweet, but I think fields are where they should stay. Actually, our house backs onto a field – a paradise for rodents. That said, I wouldn't harm any mice who chose to be our cohabitees either. So all I can do is plead with them.

> The mouse in our house is rampant, oh jeez!
> He eats our rice and nibbles on cheese;
> He weighs only ounces,
> He waits – then he pounces;
> The mouse in our house, desist, will you please!

Nature, however, has a way of exacting retribution – even if humans won't. I've already told you about my partiality to nuts and seeds, and the beauty of nuts and seeds is that you don't have to cook them. You just open a packet and gorge. Just like this mouse. Well, maybe not to quite such an extent: I'm still with you, after all.

> Having raided each larder and shop,
> This mouse did not know when to stop:
> It mused: "What I need
> Is yummy bird seed,"
> Then he polished the lot and went pop.

Poor mousie. I had also tried to write about ponies, but my ditty went horribly wrong: you can judge for yourself.

> I would rather write on ponies,
> But we have got all these cronies
> On Liz Truss's Honours List:
> That's not something you have missed?

> Also donors with their dosh;
> Folks' objections are just tosh.
> Want to rise without a glitch?
> Be a crony or be rich.

Tory cronies and donors notwithstanding, I get my love of animals from my late mum. When, over twenty-six years ago, we were moving from London to Keswick, I wanted to spare her and our two cats the worst of the hassle: packing up a whole house is a pain in the whatsit. I thus travelled with the three of them (by train) to Cumbria a few days before our house move. I put Mum in a hotel and the cats in a cattery, returning to London the same day. And this is what happened. My mum would visit the cattery every day, walking from cage to cage and talking to all the felines to lift their spirits. If felines have spirits, that is. After completing her mission one day, she made for the door – only to find it locked. Having fed their charges, the cattery people had left the place and locked the door, clearly not noticing that Mum was still there. But Mum, having survived the entire World War II in Warsaw, wasn't in the least fazed. She simply resumed her confabulations with the pussies and patiently waited for the cattery people to return with the next feed. That's the spirit.

On to larger creatures now. I have now led my lovely Roamers for over seven years. Together, we have roamed far and wide, exploring all parts of Lakeland and climbing its magnificent mountains and hills. It's amazing that they find the time and energy to join my walks. Until I myself retired, I hadn't realised how busy life in one's *genuine* prime could be. All those family commitments, grandchild-sitting duties, charitable activities and worldwide cruises. Although Vinnie and I don't do cruises and have no grandchildren (which, with no children, would be rather difficult to accomplish), we seem always to be chasing our tail, with not enough time to do all we would like to do. My books won't write themselves, that's for sure. From time to time, we look at each other and wonder how on earth we ever found the time for full-time employment. Moreover, in those days you couldn't even work from home, so there was all this daily commuting to the office to contend with. And the current workers are complaining! So this is another of my tributes to my lovely Roamers.

> Their joie de vivre is hard to top,
> They are high-octane and never stop;
> They keep, with great flair,
> Those balls in the air,
> Not allowing one *ever* to drop!

What's more, they don't seem to have been put off by all the traps I have led them into – albeit inadvertently. Obviously, I can't recount the mishaps I've already told you about: if you are paying £8.99 – but, who knows, my publisher may even up the price of this one to £9.99 (inflation still hasn't been tamed, after all) – you expect new content, not some regurgitated stuff. Despite everything, however, my lovely Roamers seem to adore me. Genuinely. At least that's what I had imagined until the disappointing truth finally dawned on me. But before the scales fell from my eyes, imagine my delight on being regularly called great, brilliant, splendid, fabulous and similarly effusive things. Goodness me, my ego, hitherto battered and bruised, started reflating rather rapidly and was, in fact, in danger of going pop – just like this greedy mouse.

Thankfully, before this calamity occurred, I realised that this was merely the case of a missing comma. You see, when I plan and organise walks, I communicate with my lovely Roamers by email. I tell them all about each walk, give them the mileage – estimated with the help from my trusty string, of course – and then make car-sharing arrangements: unless we use buses, we share cars to do our bit for the planet. So I get lots of email responses which go like this: great Anna, brilliant Anna, splendid Anna, etc., etc. You are not going to tell me that your ego would remain unaffected, are you? Alas, they were merely expressing their approval for my plans, as in:

Great, Anna!
Brilliant, Anna!
Splendid, Anna!
Etc., etc., etc.

And it was the absence of this comma that fed my illusions of greatness – at least for a while. Here are a few more examples of how the presence or absence of the comma can alter the meaning of a phrase or sentence.

Kill, Rex!
Kill Rex!

They are attacking, Dave.
They are attacking Dave.

These are good, folk.
These are good folk.

Take this, Boris.
Take this Boris. (I wouldn't take this Boris if you paid me big bucks.)

Follow them, guys.

Follow them guys. (Yep, the grammar here is a tad dodgy, but we've all heard, and read, similar commands.)

Let's eat, Granny.
Let's eat Granny.

In other words, the comma should be used when we address somebody or something in writing. Now, have you noticed what I've just done? I have smuggled a bit of grammar in here – yippee! Admittedly, the use of the comma, and of other punctuation marks, is the province of punctuation, but punctuation is governed by grammar to a very large extent. Honestly. So don't believe those who tell you that you put the comma where you have pauses in speech. Yes, this does happen, but it's only a small part of the picture. Worse still, some will tell you that you don't need punctuation at all or that you can put punctuation marks wherever you like. Bunkum! The role of punctuation is to make your writing as clear and unambiguous as possible so that you don't end up eating your granny.

And grammar is your guide here: those clause elements which are closely related to each other don't get separated by a comma (or other punctuation marks), while those which are more peripheral to the rest of the clause do. The former are central clause elements, namely the subject, the verb, the object and the complement and the latter the adverbial – a multi-faceted category. But if this knowledge is to be of any practical use, one needs to be able to identify these clause elements in the first place. Regrettably, this is where I have to leave this fascinating subject if this book is to avoid the sorry destiny of all these political party manifestos and end up in the bin. But I hope that the publishers of academic books, and of those which aspire to covering English grammar in a light-hearted way, have taken the bait. Come on, guys, what I don't know about English grammar (alongside public transport) isn't worth knowing. I have amassed thousands of funny examples of incorrect usage so can make my grammatical books entertaining. Honest!

Returning to my lovely Roamers, even though they don't, after all, think I am brilliant, they nevertheless stick with me, and we continue enjoying convivial walks. Moreover, I'm no longer distraught when they address me as 'sorry Anna' when they inform me by email that they won't be joining my ramble. Because I know that they are merely trying to say 'sorry, Anna'. So I love them regardless. I can't think of a better place to present a few more to you. (I daren't say where I introduced the first batch.)

Julie is our quiz mistress, who has put me to shame. I'm supposed to be this great big expert on the Lakeland mountains but couldn't work out the anagrams for any of our fells during the gala lunch celebrating the tenth anniversary of our u3a. Julie, on the other hand, cracked them all and scooped the first prize. And she offers me fascinating insights into life in Germany, where she resides for a part of the year. Before her surgery there, the German medics apologised most sincerely for the wait she would have to endure. Its length? Six *weeks*!

Julie

Our lovely Roamer Julie
Tackles our quizzes cooly:
Every anagram
Is soon figured – wham!
We think she is great – she is, truly.

Jo is one of those Roamers who have scaled all the Lakeland fells – after conquering the Himalayas (although the latter feat has been accomplished by her alone). She is always cheerful and great company on all our walks.

Jo

Lovely Jo? She's widely known
Never to protest or moan;
She cycles and climbs –
In one day sometimes,
And she is always in the zone!

Like Jo, Jennie is a keen cyclist – as well as being an excellent climber and a talented painter. And she greatly helped me with procuring my new hip (long story) – a true friend!

Jennie

She takes hurdles in her stride
When she's on a cycle ride;
She does love her art,
Is helpful and smart
And will roam on our fells far and wide.

Olga is one of our globetrotters yet, somehow, manages to join many of my walks, which she always enlivens with the stories of her travels. And of the amazing aquatic life on her doorstep: her Keswick lodge sits right by Derwentwater. What's more, she spoke to King Charles – then Prince – when he visited Keswick to add a touch of splendour to the celebrations after the Lake District had become a UNESCO World Heritage Site.

Olga

> When you call her, she's rarely at home,
> Her globetrotting could fill up a tome
> And inspire droll ditties:
> She does mountains, lakes, cities –
> If it's Friday, it must surely be Rome!

Tricia and Sara are delightful Roamers who are always great company and whose humour sizzles and sparkles. Moreover, they kindly agreed to accompany me on the climb of Wasdale Red Pike, which was the last mountain to have been scaled by me for the ninth time. How they can manage to drive along our narrow and bendy roads with such panache is beyond me.

Tricia and Sara

> Tricia and Sara come in a pair:
> We all agree both maidens are fair;
> They ramble with us –
> Their humour a plus,
> Their vim and their vigour quite rare.

Like me, Paul is an animal lover, and he joins our walks whenever his canines allow him some time off. His lovely wife, Paddy, also has some say in the matter, of course. And if you could only be a fly on the wall when we talk politics – then again, mountains have no walls, but you undoubtedly get my drift.

Paul

> We are fond of our Paul,
> Who will always stand quite tall;
> Whenever he can,
> He'll climb with my clan;
> Mountains hold him in their thrall.

There can't be many corners of the globe not visited, or many mountains not scaled, by Celia and Stuart, who are also expert rock climbers. Whenever they join our walk, we are delighted, for their schedule is truly jam-packed – more hectic than even that of our perambulating feline, Finn.

Celia and Stuart

> They've both travelled much, and they are
> Most seasoned explorers by far;
> Rock climbing they do:
> Our Celia and Stu;
> Put simply, each one is a star.

At long last, I have somebody else with a foreign accent in

my group – and another linguist at that! I mean Christine, who is French. Both she and her husband, Adam, are great walkers, and I am delighted that they have joined my group. My conversations with Christine on the intricacies of English grammar are a real treat – and a rare one at that: I daren't raise the subject with native English speakers (with the exception of Moira, perhaps).

Christine and Adam

Our Adam and Christine
Both possess a climbing gene;
She's a linguist – French,
He's good with a wrench;
We're happy with them on the scene.

As well as being an excellent walker, Moira is also fabulous company. I get so engrossed in our fascinating linguistic and political confabulations that I can easily forget where I'm supposed to be going. And what she doesn't know about Britain's fauna and flora is not worth knowing: a walking encyclopaedia!

Moira

She knows all 'bout trees and flowers,
Can entrance us all for hours;
She shares my world-view
And loves grammar too;
We're delighted she is ours!

Jane is another delightful Roamer. I am deeply honoured to have this lovely lady drive all the way from Bowness (which is in the south Lakes – we are in the north) just to join my walks. The membership secretary of our u3a is astonished that someone living that far away has chosen to be one of my Roamers. And, whenever Jane is hiking with us, her relaxed demeanour and gentle manner are a real tonic.

Jane

She lives very far away
But does join my walks – wehey!
She climbs like a dream,
Is part of our team;
Our love for her grows day by day.

Gaynor and Dave are yet another lovely couple whose presence on my walks always makes these rambles extra-special. Gaynor, who is a retired GP, saved me from a meltdown when she cautioned me against self-diagnosing a terminal condition after I had discovered that my potassium levels were sky-high. She was right, of course!

Gaynor and Dave

Gaynor's married to kind Dave,
Both those hikers are our fave:
Each of them so nice,
She gives sage advice;
They do thus deserve a rave.

Heather is another retired GP who has dealt expertly, and patiently, with my medical queries. And Brian's groundbreaking scientific discoveries have saved countless lives. As you can see, my group is full of brainboxes – aren't I lucky! And, just like all my Roamers, Heather and Brian are great climbers, having scaled innumerable mountains rather than just Harter Fell – but it was *extremely* hot that day.

Heather and Brian

> They are both extremely smart,
> But they also have a heart;
> They did very well
> To bag Harter Fell;
> Without them, we'd fall apart!

Deborah and Paul are the latest addition to my group – and what a marvellous addition! Being new to the Lake District, they infect the rest of us with their unbounded enthusiasm, and I am over the moon to be able to contribute, in however small a way, to their exploration of the area.

Deborah and Paul

> They are very nice, and, though new,
> They do resonate with our crew;
> They have what it takes
> And love our Lakes,
> Enjoying the walks which we do.

15

Convivial Walks, Unexpected Animal Encounters and the Geological Disposal Facility

Returning to convivial walks with my lovely Roamers, let's take this one, which started at the northern tip of Thirlmere, a large reservoir south of Keswick. As we were crossing the reservoir's dam, wispy mist was swirling around, but the vibrant autumnal colours were dazzling in their intensity nevertheless. Soon, we found ourselves at the foot of the steep afforested slope culminating on the ridge between Benn Man and Raven Crag and commenced our ascent along the declivitous route. Halfway up, a very pleasant forest road intersecting the slope provided a welcome respite, its gradient being much gentler. We were thus able to concentrate on admiring the magnificent display of reds, scarlets, browns, russets, yellows, goldens, oranges and greys decorating the surrounding trees and shrubs – a truly breathtaking sight. And, through the trees, we could catch a glimpse of the calm waters of Thirlmere at our feet. To lengthen what would otherwise have been a relatively short walk, I then gave my charges a bit of a runaround by sticking with the forest road, which, having reached the altitude of Benn Man, decided that it would be a good idea to plunge right down. Having lost quite a bit of height, we eventually started climbing again, emerging at the foot of Raven Crag. An excellent, partially stepped, path then led us to the summit, which, at that point, was swathed in thick mist. After retracting our steps to the bottom of the crag, we visited Castle Crag Fort, dramatically perched high above the deep ravine of Shoulthwaite Gill. The descent made use of excellent forest tracks, which conveyed us down to the edge of Shoulthwaite Moss. The final section led across the fields towards Bridge End Farm, now clearly visible on the other side of the attractive old bridge suspended over St John's Beck immediately ahead.

Suddenly, a shock: just past the bridge, and right by the footpath, stood a most ginormous bull. What now? Unfortunately, there was no way of bypassing the milky-coloured beast, and there ensued a heated debate as to whom the animal might choose to charge first. Apparently, the colour most likely to get them going was red, and two of our gents were wearing bright-red parka jackets. So should we shield them by throwing a protective ring around them – much as Matt Hancock had done with our care homes at the beginning of the Covid pandemic? According to his, entirely unbiased, version of events, that is. Or should we, perhaps, sacrifice the guys so that the rest of us could escape unscathed? Look, Johnson & Co were, allegedly, prepared to sacrifice thousands of people, and here we were talking about two only. Besides, you take the lead from those higher up in the pecking order. As we were thus deliberating, Jo, the daintiest of our fair ladies, surged forth in a most intrepid fashion. Oh, no! Petrified, we all held our breath, but the listless bovine failed to stir, appearing entirely uninterested in the goings-on around it. Emboldened, we plucked up enough courage to follow our audacious friend, reaching the next gate in record-quick time. I'd say of Usain Bolt's standard. Thus ended one of our unexpected encounters with animals.

Another occurred during our hike taking in Lank Rigg, Crag Fell & Grike in the Western Fells. We started near the Kinniside Stone Circle, which was, apparently, painstakingly restored to its original glory after having been dismantled by local farmers. From there, Coldfell Road, a handy shortcut for Sellafield, provided an easy passage to the sprawling moorland of Kinniside Common, dominated by the lonely outpost of Lank Rigg – the day's first objective. The famous A. Wainwright described this vast grassy area as 'a place of sheep and singing larks', and, indeed, there was ample evidence of both, enhancing the tranquillity of the scene.

> Not a cirrus in the sky
> As you amble slowly by
> In a pensive mood,
> Loving solitude,
> With the skylarks larking high.

Although I wasn't by myself on that occasion, the peacefulness of the scene was nevertheless very soothing.

Our meditative mood was, however, somewhat disturbed by the sight of a large herd of cattle, which had evidently decided that the best place to graze that very morning was right by the bridleway at the point where it crossed the River Calder. Since the crossing needed to be negotiated somehow, we sought guidance from a farming expert in our midst, who advised us that you must never try to flee from an advancing bovine. Instead, you must look it boldly in the eye, make yourself as large as possible and shout, "Shoo, shoo, shoo!" Mercifully, however, the herd simply got on with their mechanistic munching, clearly disinclined to mount a charge – just like our bull. The veracity of this particular instruction has thus remained unproven. After this encounter, we proceeded unimpeded all the way to the sprawling summit of the bulky Lank Rigg, although the sheep grazing in this unfrequented area were, clearly, intrigued by our presence. From our vantage point, trying to identify the fells framing the picture proved an interesting challenge, but Seatallan, Caw Fell, Haycock and Scafell were among the recognised fells. And, looking west towards the coast, one couldn't fail to notice Sellafield, its industrial structures glistening in the sun.

Ah, Sellafield! Currently a nuclear decommissioning plant, it is rumoured to be the most polluted industrial site in Western Europe. Right on our doorstep – quite a distinction. Sellafield has to deal with the legacy of Calder Hall, the world's first nuclear power station, which produced not only weapons-grade plutonium and electricity but also lots and lots of extremely dangerous nuclear waste. So Sellafield is reprocessing all this waste – plus some which has since been imported from the countries eager to dump their hazardous refuse on someone else's doorstep. But the stuff is so dangerous that the scientific consensus is that it should ultimately be stored deep underground – apparently the only genuinely safe mode of storage. They call it a Geological Disposal Facility (GDF). So they have been looking for the best place to junk all this waste. But this place has to have suitable geology. They say that clay is the most suitable – but would you shove your nuclear waste under London? So they are trying to dump it in Cumbria. Because Cumbria doesn't have quite so many inhabitants, and those it does have are supposed to be pliant. Pliant? *In Keswick*? Full of retired professors, brain surgeons and aerospace engineers? And writers. Although writers never retire. Just like the Pope. Look at me. The Nuclear Decommissioning Authority had better organise a fact-finding mission to Keswick. Sharpish. Be that as it may, what Cumbria also doesn't have is suitable geology: they had been trying to identify a safe disposal site here *for decades* – to no avail. So they have changed the goalposts, promised to bribe the local populace and continue to keep their focus on our county. Because other places in Britain don't want a GDF on their doorstep – would *you*?

> Looking right and looking left:
> Where to site a GDF?
> This might not be to your taste,
> But we've lots and lots of waste –
> Radioactive – in our store –
> And we're getting even more!

It's a shame – yes, this we grant –
That the reprocessing plant
In West Cumbria, by the sea,
Gives us grief – we all agree –
Full of highly toxic trash,
Missing targets, leeching cash.

So we are in quite a bind,
For we must – we *have to* – find
Somewhere quiet up the road
To conceal the deadly load;
Somewhere quiet – out of sight;
We are *certain* we are right.

Our waste is safe for now,
But it must be moved somehow.
Where to? This is what we've found:
A large chamber in the ground
Should be dug (it should, we swear)
And the waste be buried there.

Chamber's fine, but experts say
That it's safest dug in clay
And that it is very clear
There is nowhere safe up here;
Our locals? They've said "no":
For them, Lakeland is no go.

> Problem is (and it's a beast):
> You want clay – you go south-east,
> This, though, we can't entertain:
> Choosing London? That's insane!
> It's far too important, and
> This is why it will be shunned.
>
> We must choose a place where we
> Get the locals to agree;
> No one wants our waste? We know,
> But we have a lot of dough,
> Safety can be got around
> And dissenting voices drowned;
>
> Even if terrain's no good,
> We can bribe the neighbourhood;
> There's no need to hit the roof:
> Our stratagem? Foolproof;
> We're relaxed, we're quite at ease:
> We will do just as we please.

It will be interesting to see what happens. Back to our hike. After Lank Rigg, it was uneventful: having scaled Crag Fell, we admired the spectacular view of Ennerdale Lake, stretching out at our feet and set among the soaring fells, the mighty Pillar being foremost among them. No, it was *genuinely* foremost – unlike our Foremost Authority. After climbing Grike, we returned along a pleasant bridleway which descended to Coldfell Road across the lower slopes of Blakeley Rise, partially covered by the verdant Heckbarley plantation – a welcome feature in those otherwise bare surroundings. That would have been it had our return route not been blocked off by a large herd of wild horses which usually graze in the area. These ones, however, stood determinedly right in the middle of the road. Given that we were already in our cars, the drivers hooted, tooted and blared, but the impassive beasts refused to budge. So we wound down our windows and started waving our arms about – to no avail. We then shouted as loudly as we could, but all we got in response were the energetic swishes of the immobile beasts' tails. Finally, we managed to drive around them by manoeuvring the cars along the wide, albeit bumpy, road verges – and I got this limerick out of our encounter.

> This horsie had a chestnut mane,
> But flies were his perennial bane:
> He had to unleash
> His tail with a swish;
> Now, flies, who is feeling the pain?

Talking of horses, as Vinnie and I were descending from our nearby fell, Walla Crag, on a wet afternoon, we were followed by three huge specimens which, for some reason, had been left grazing by the touristy path by the farmer. The slope was steep, and the animals were right behind us, one practically nibbling at my rucksack. Quite intimidating. We sped up, and so did they, one slipping on the wet grass and sliding on his knees. But he was soon up and in hot pursuit again. At this point, Vinnie inserted himself valiantly between the beast and me, and I desperately tried to remember where he kept his will.

Needless to say, we were mightily relieved to have reached the gate at the bottom, which we managed to fasten just in time – phew.

There were other unexpected animal encounters, of course, but I wouldn't want to go on for too long lest I bore you to death. I'll just tell you about two brief run-ins with dogs. Don't get me wrong: I love dogs. But, while some love me back, others don't. Such as this one. You can do a fabulous linear walk from Great Langdale to Borrowdale over Stake Pass and then along Langstrath. You get yourself to Great Langdale by using two buses and then pick up your return transport at Rosthwaite. So I am descending from the broad plateau of Stake Pass into Langstrath along the fantastic zig-zag path which cuts out the slope's steepness most effectively. And climbing towards me are a couple accompanied by an unleashed dog. Suddenly, the canine jumps up and bites me on the hand. Several times. Luckily, I am wearing gloves, but the experience isn't pleasant. The couple, however, just stand there impassively and simply observe the unfolding scene. And when I suggest that they ought to keep their unruly canine on the lead, the lady shrugs her shoulders and announces: "She doesn't like sticks." *She doesn't like sticks?* But all the other walkers are using walking sticks, so it's all the more reason for the couple to restrain their pet. And when I bump into them later, the dog still isn't on the lead.

> It is something of a puzzle:
> This dog bites but has no muzzle;
> If the owners are pea-brained,
> It is they who should be trained.

Another dog's ardour towards me, however, couldn't be cooled. Unfortunately, this ardour found its manifestation at the very top of the ridge leading from the summit of Grisedale Pike down to the village of Braithwaite. The ridge is rather narrow at this point and has some scrambly bits, so being jumped on by a very large canine was quite an unsettling experience – despite the creature's clear amorous intentions. So, as I teeter there precariously, I scream, the dog's owners holler and the other walkers yell. Quite a hoo-ha. Mercifully, I didn't tumble from the ridge – it was a *long* way down – and the owners managed to pull the beastie off me. Whereupon, they put it on the lead. An example to others – particularly the Stake Pass couple. Which seems an excellent note on which to end this chapter.

16

Disintegrated Investigators, Sliced Cars, a Reproductive Feat of the Year, Destructive Forecasters and Other Dangling Participles

I think it may now be safe for me to indulge in a brief grammatical interlude. I've been good so far, haven't I? Anyway, it's my book, so, if I want to slip some grammar in here, who is to stop me? Besides, Moira, who is one of my delightful Roamers and who also loves grammar, said that she had hugely enjoyed the *Sunday Times* howler quoted by me in Book 1 (that about parents divorcing at the age of six), adding that she would have liked more similar examples. So this chapter is dedicated to you, Moira.

Apropos grammar, this book is literally bursting with it, of course, because grammar organises every single phrase, clause and sentence, helping language users to communicate their meaning clearly and to create the intended effect. And what could be worse than unintentionally provoking howls of laughter when you are trying to convey a serious message? This is, however, what happens when you misrelate your participles.

Misrelated participles constitute a grammatical blunder which can be traced back to the works of Chaucer and Shakespeare and which has been generously sprinkled throughout the writing of many authors over centuries. Despite having been lambasted by grammarians for more than a hundred years, the error is alive and kicking in today's literature, media, education, public life and even academia. And don't even get me started on those who were never taught English grammar. The blunder certainly has the potential to be one of the most amusing grammatical lapses around, although there are undoubtedly other worthy contenders. Their exposure will, however, have to wait until some publisher commissions me to write my funny book on grammar.

Misrelated participles are also called unattached, unrelated, disconnected, suspended, pendant, hanging and dangling – among other things. I usually say dangling participles – or danglers, for short – because of the evocativeness of this phrase: what you are looking at is a participle dangling hopelessly without its proper partner and, in sheer despair, latching on to the wrong word and creating communicative havoc in the process.

Having been researching grammatical lapses in the writing of native English speakers for over a quarter of a century, I have amassed hundreds of unintentionally hilarious examples of dangling participles – all culled from so-called reputable sources. I am, however, determined to exercise utmost restraint here – not easy for a creature of passions – and will offer you a mere handful of examples. In each, the participle is italicised; you will know it as soon as you see it. And, in line with the practice widely adopted in linguistics, the asterisk (*) at the front signals incorrect usage.

First of all, let's look at participles incorrectly referring to an earlier context.

> *After *disintegrating* at an altitude of 39 miles, the investigators face a difficult task. *(ITV1)*

Just imagine those poor disintegrated investigators! Do you think ITV1 was hinting at their miraculous resurrection? That would be news indeed! But the hapless TV channel clearly hadn't realised that a participle such as *disintegrating* can be made to refer to other words *only* within the confines of its own sentence. This means that such initially placed participles are forward-looking. Just like you. Any attempts – and they are frequent – to relate them to an earlier context are doomed to failure, the resulting messages being nonsensical, ambiguous, misleading, unintentionally hilarious or downright unintelligible. Such blunders cannot usually be corrected without knowing what has been said in the preceding sentence. In this instance, what had been mentioned earlier was the American shuttle Columbia, so it was *the shuttle* that had disintegrated – *not* the investigators. This sentence should thus have read:

> Since it [OR Columbia] disintegrated at an altitude of 39 miles, the investigators face a difficult task.

OR

> It [OR Columbia] *having disintegrated* at an altitude of 39 miles, the investigators face a difficult task.

Here is another example of a dangler latching onto the wrong word simply because the right one doesn't appear in its sentence.

> **Sliced* in two by a busy road, the cars run into hundreds.
> *(BBC Two)*

Much as I love the BBC, I am compelled to report that it has contributed to my vast collection of howlers. In this particular programme, the anchor, clearly oblivious to the dangling participle trap, was earlier talking about a forecourt packed full of hundreds of used cars for sale. This is why the correct version of this sentence goes like this.

> *Sliced* in two by a busy road, the forecourt is packed with hundreds of cars.

The grammatical rule governing participial attachment is as follows: just like all initially placed participles, those incorrectly referring to an earlier context are *always* interpreted as referring to *the subject of the clause which governs them*. And such a clause will *always* appear *in the same sentence* – not earlier. In other words, initial participles must obey *the subject-attachment rule*. It is an inviolable principle, which is, however, frequently violated.

> Your position will be abject
> If you can't pinpoint the subject:
> You will trip and, in your tangle,
> Make your participles dangle.

Now, I can hear you say that sentences usually appear in context and that you can work out the intended meaning from this context. A red herring if ever there was one! By the way, when I first came to this wonderful country, I marvelled at the diversity of its fauna: our Polish herring was usually silvery. Then again, Britain seemed to me amazing, so why wouldn't it have amazing marine life as well? But I have since learnt what it meant. Back to engaging in language guesswork, remember that communication is not only about conveying the intended meaning but also about creating the desired effect. Would you write in a scientific paper 'we *was* [sic] *venimently* [sic] opposed to *there* [sic] *finding's* [sic]', in an article in *The Times* 'the Prime Minister should *of* [sic] cut our *tax's* [sic] or in a school textbook '*students'* [sic] should learn *them* [sic] *principals* [sic] of *grammer* [sic]'? Why not? We can all understand the intended meaning, after all. So this argument doesn't hold water.

In the following, nonsensical, sentences – all authentic and all perpetrated by apparently well-educated offenders – initial participles have been made to refer – incorrectly – to what had been said before. Because I'm not going to tell you what that was, you are going to have to guess, but it is possible. And, I hope, great fun. You may not be able to figure out to what *exactly* each initial participle is meant to refer, but you can certainly get close.

*Launching into a clear blue Florida sky, thousands gathered to watch the blast. *(BBC Radio 2)*

Launching thousands of people into space must have been an incredible spectacle! What do you think could have been launched?

*Having gone through the exhausting palaver of giving birth, the boyfriend still did not feel compelled to do the decent thing. *(The Sunday Times)*

This exhausted boyfriend must have made medical history.

*Conceived by the British Council, the delegates will visit China. *(The British Council)*

In quoting this howler, *The Sunday Times* called it a reproductive feat of the year – too right! What do you think was *really* conceived by the British Council?

*Killed in the park by a stranger, the killer is jailed for life today. *(ITV1)*

This is surely a case of a miraculous resurrection.

**Once *legalised* in the 80s, thousands of children got the bug. *(BBC Two)*

It's always good for children to be legalised. The meaning of this sentence you wouldn't be able to guess if you tried, though: they meant a CB radio.

*After *conducting* eight autopsies, only one patient was found to be entirely free of the protein. *(The Economist)*

They let *the patient* conduct autopsies? Our pathology service, like the rest of the NHS, must be truly on its knees.

**Dwarfed* by the American economy, Canadian officials adopt US regulations wholesale. *(The Daily Telegraph)*

I am sure that the American economy dwarfs far more than Canadian officials.

*Initially *valued* at £160,000, Williams then spent £3,000 on new lighting and flooring and a new front door. *(The Sunday Times)*

Blimey, I wouldn't let anyone value me so cheaply! Then again, if you consider the price of my books…

*Once *set up*, an investor has a year to choose where to invest. *(The Independent)*

I don't like being set up so can only feel sorry for this investor.

*While *clarifying* by phone that this was a fraudulent order, my doorbell rang. *(The Daily Telegraph)*

This must have been one of these smart doorbells capable of doing absolutely everything – just like my Facebook friend's gizmos.

> **Placed* into special measures, Ofsted inspectors found pupil behaviour poor.
> *(The Times Educational Supplement)*

Having had the dubious pleasure of scrutinising error-ridden Ofsted inspectors' reports as the so-called quality reader contracted by the schools' inspectorate while I ran my own educational consultancy from Keswick, I wouldn't be at all surprised if one or two inspectors were themselves placed in special measures. But, of course, the hapless author simply got his, or her, participle in a twist.

> * *Married* to Ian, they have two daughters.
> *(The Sunday Times)*

Are they *both* married to Ian? I thought that bigamy was illegal in this wonderful country. This one is quite easy to guess, though. Now, I think that these few examples of participles incorrectly attached to words for the previous sentence will have to do if this chapter is not to balloon into a whole book. Actually, one book would not be enough to cover all howlers involving participles, but that's my project for the future: one needs a goal in life – even at my age.

Back to the here and now, however: initial participles also get misrelated within the confines of their own sentence – an even more frequent error. Such sentences are far easier to correct because the word to which the dangling participle is meant to refer is already there, so all you need to do is rearrange the sentence. In the corrected (un-asterisked) sentences given below, the subject to which the participle should attach itself has been both emboldened and italicised.

*After *leaving* a trail of destruction, forecasters predict the rain will continue. *(BBC One)*

Just when one thought that weather forecasters were always perfectly behaved. The conduct of our favourite, Paul Mooney, is certainly always impeccable, and he would never wreck the studio! But what the unfortunate BBC anchor was attempting to say was this:

After *leaving* a trail of destruction, **the rain**, forecasters predict, will continue.

OR

After *leaving* a trail of destruction, **the rain** will continue, predict forecasters.

And how about this gem?

*Morphined up to the hilt, the nurses later told me I went into the operating theatre singing Bowie's *Rock'n'Roll Suicide*. *(The Sunday Times)*

As if our poor beleaguered NHS didn't have enough problems, it now has to contend with nurses off their head on morphine! The intention, however, was this:

Morphined up to the hilt, *I* was later told by the nurses that I had gone into the operating theatre singing Bowie's *Rock'n'Roll Suicide*.

As I've said, I have collected literally hundreds of similar examples, a handful of which is given below. Because the initial participle in each is misrelated within its own sentence, you should be able to correct each blunder with ease. As before, have fun!

**Found* dead in her bed, tonight her uncle is under arrest. (ITV1)*

Another scoop by ITV1: a second miraculous resurrection!

*Murdered for refusing to join the gang, the mother of the schoolboy speaks out today. *(ITV1)*

And a third! Surely, the channel qualifies for the Scoop of the Year Award!

**If *found* guilty, his lawyers are going to plead insanity. (BBC One)*

You have to watch these cunning lawyers.

**Virtually *untouched* for 3,000 years, Howard Carter discovered the statues in the tomb of Tutankhamun. (Channel 4)*

I'm sure Howard Carter was glad to have been left untouched for 3,000 years.

**When *delivered* in a fresh, artistic way, children will seize on writing. (The Times Educational Supplement)*

This is by far the best way to deliver children, if you ask me.

*Once *activated*, you will be able to access The Journal. (Cambridge University Press)

I must say that this particular assurance got me well and truly activated!

*Slowly *cooked* in the oven, you might expect vegetables to be healthy. (The Daily Mail)

Isn't this shocking? Even a lobster gets a kinder treatment than you: boiling water will kill you far quicker than being slowly cooked.

**Walking* to a minicab rank, my bottom was vigorously patted. (The Sunday Times)

This is what happens when you let a bottom wander alone at night.

*Once *anaesthetised*, Patrick started operating on her. (Channel 5)

So not only are patients now called on to perform autopsies, but they are also allowed to operate on others – and under anaesthetic at that. God help us!

*ptml>*Growing up*, my mother had a very wealthy boyfriend. (The Sunday Times)

Isn't it a bit early for boyfriends? Unless this mother was a Lolita.

> *Lying* in state, thousands pay their respects to Nelson Mandela. *(BBC One)*

I wonder how they managed to get thousands of the deceased to lie in state all at the same time…

> *Begun* by pagans, *kept* alive by peasants, Rupert Christiansen traces the surprising origins of our favourite seasonal songs. *(The Daily Telegraph)*

I bet Rupert Christiansen was relieved to have been kept alive by peasants – even if he was begun by pagans.

> *Last used* for storage, the owner will be taking a gamble on whether or not the council will grant permission to convert the property to residential use. *(The Sunday Times)*

I imagine the new owner found it somewhat uncomfortable to be used for storage. Much as I am tempted to go on and on, I have to force myself to exercise restraint: one grammatical chapter, and that's your lot in this book. But there will be others. Books, I mean.

To reiterate, just like initial participles incorrectly referring to an earlier context, those misrelated within their own sentences must be made to refer to *the subject of the clause which governs them.* You will now be aware that this important principle is called *the subject-attachment rule*. This is the briefest of snapshots of initial dangling participles, but participles sitting further down their sentence also get regularly mishandled. And participles are by no means the only victims of such unceremonious treatment, for all sorts of other constructions can also wreak communicative havoc in unpractised hands. Take 'as' meaning 'in the capacity of', which is another classic. Look at this (courtesy of the BBC)!

> **As a mother of eight*, the Fuhrer awarded me the Cross of Honour.

One can only hope that the Fuhrer didn't find childbirth too traumatic. Admittedly, a blunder such as this isn't easy to top – but this definitely takes me beyond the remit of this book. I'm open to offers from publishers, though!

> "Aged six, Susan's mother, quite tragically, died."
> "That's awful, poor Susan – the girl must have cried."
> "This is not the point, though, just think – can't you see?"
> "This *must* be the point – I cannot agree."

> "No, no, it's their grammar, it's wrong (déjà vu);
> They often get muddled – believe me, it's true:
> They said that *the mother* was six – what a laugh!"
> "But aren't they natives? They do this?" "Not half!

> "*Aged* here is a dangler – it is, on my life:
> It is misrelated: this error is rife."
> "*A dangler?*" "This *aged* – it needed a match
> But found the wrong noun to which to attach."

"So what's the right way?" "*Aged* six, *Susan* lost…"
"Her mum?" "That's correct – my heart has been crossed."
"I see, but they don't?" "Some do not indeed:
A long time ago, it had been decreed

"That kids don't need grammar." "*You what?*" "Sadly, yes."
"That's bonkers!" "I know – it ends in a mess;
But some of us, aliens, in this glorious land
Adore English grammar – and we are on hand!"

17

The Wrong Type of Snow, Quiet Coaches, Unwanted Gifts and Christmas Carp

With Christmas fast approaching (provided I have timed this book right), I have decided to imbue my final lark with the Yuletide theme. Earlier on, I devoted quite a bit of space to Christmas – after all, it's such a huge thing in Britain – but this chapter will have a decidedly Polish flavour. What do you mean this *entire* book has a Polish flavour? I haven't been sufficiently British for you? In that case, I might as well stop trying. Actually, there is a certain amount of freedom in letting go. You will see the difference in these two chapters, honest: they are quite unlike the rest of the book. Apart from the previous chapter, which was also unlike anything else. So maybe this rollercoaster ride has nothing to do with my letting go, after all…

Be that as it may, let me introduce you to two of my Polish relatives. The ones I didn't wish to speak of in Chapter 3. They are my granny Czeslawa and my young cousin Zdzislawa; both are paying Vinnie and me a visit in Keswick en route to Florida. Granny's arthritis isn't getting any better but does improve in warm weather. And my young cousin acts as her travelling companion. What do you mean I'm too old to have a granny? You think that only Britain has teenage mothers? That's Granny's bloodline. Anyway, she isn't my *proper* granny; I think Britons call this level of kinship third cousin twice removed, but I'm not going to call her this, am I? By the way, she and Zdzislawa weren't going to stay with us over Christmas – would *you* if Florida beckoned? – but we are currently on our fifth rail strike of the year, so they can't get to the airport. Actually, even if they could, we are currently on our fourth airline strike of the year, so they wouldn't be able to fly out. I have to confess that the poor lambs are a bit traumatised: their train journey from Heathrow to Penrith (via London, of course) had been severely delayed because of the wrong type of snow on the line. But at least this made a change from the leaves on the line, which had delayed them during their previous visit. Strangely, my relatives don't seem to appreciate that change can be quite refreshing. Can't think why. As for snow, in the Poland of my youth we used to get tons and tons of it, but I can't recall there ever having fallen even one snowflake of the wrong type – *ever*. So some things were actually fine even under communism.

On the plus side, Granny and Zdzislawa had, on my advice, chosen to travel from London to Penrith in a quiet coach so were not surrounded by people yelling into their mobile phone: "I'm on the train!" or sharing, always in a very loud voice, the most intimate details of their latest romantic encounter or bust-up with a significant other. These quiet coaches really are an excellent idea, although things don't always work out as intended. After settling in Keswick, I set up my own educational and linguistic consultancy – there aren't many graduate jobs around – and my work involved quite a bit of travelling to various meetings (and then, unsurprisingly, from said meetings). Once, when I was returning home in a quiet coach (naturally), the entire journey proceeded to the soundtrack of piercing screams of some infant, blissfully unaware of the constrains imposed by such a coach. Why the mother would have chosen to travel in it I have no idea – maybe she didn't like the sound of other screaming infants either – but nobody dared say anything, and I arrived home with a thumping headache. And an even deeper conviction that I had done the right thing by choosing to remain child-free.

This is why being able to travel in a quiet coach had always been my key requirement. You won't thus be surprised by my enquiry directed at a functionary of ScotRail. But, first, I might have mentioned that, in my professional career in Britain, I'd had many incarnations. One of them was being a developer of the Scottish Curriculum of Excellence. Yes, I agree, they must have been desperate. Anyway, they did employ me. Although the job was supposed to be home-based (I was already living in the Lake District), it involved a lot of travel throughout Scotland: before I knew what to put in the new Scottish qualifications, I had to ask lots and lots of Scottish teachers. So here I am, at the Queen Street railway station in Glasgow, about to board my train, which would take me into the deepest recesses of Scotland. Naturally, I approach one of the operatives with the question as to where, at the platform, the quiet coach might be positioned. He shoots me a startled look before announcing: "All our coaches are quiet – they are double-glazed." It took all my resolve not to laugh in his face. This chasm between England and Scotland was, clearly, deeper than I had imagined.

Returning to my Polish relatives, Granny and Zdzislawa were now stuck with us for a while longer. And Granny was fretting. Not like her to fret at all, but she was doing now.

"I'd better do some Christmas shopping soon, lassie. I didn't know we were staying here over Christmas, so I hadn't got you any Christmas presents."

"Don't worry, Granny, we don't bother with Christmas presents much."

"You don't?"

"No; they have a big problem with Christmas here, you see."

"They eat and drink too much, you mean?"

"No, no, I mean yes, people do – but I meant a problem with unwanted presents."

"*Unwanted* presents?"

"Yep; they spend more than two billion pounds on unwanted Christmas presents."

"So why do they buy unwanted presents in the first place?"

"Well, they don't buy unwanted presents *on purpose*; it's just that they don't always get it right. More than two-thirds of people are given gifts they don't like."

"That's an awful lot of people, lassie."

"It is, Granny. But Vinnie and I have this rule: the only Christmas presents we ever buy for each other are books.

And there are just the two of us, so we don't buy, or get, any other presents. Easy-peasy."

At this point, I feel compelled to offer my British-born readers a revealing glimpse into the Polish culture. Even now, the Polish Christmas is a far more intimate affair than the usual western jamboree: Granny has told me. A small cluster of close relatives gathered by whatever source of heat is available, a glass of Bison Grass Vodka in hand and a slice of poppy seed cake on the plate – that sort of thing. I mean after the main meal, which will be described in a bit. There might also be the odd alcohol-fuelled fight, but we will draw a veil over such unseemly incidents. But Christmas is, in essence, the time for only the immediate family to come together, and presents are purchased accordingly. There is no running around like headless chickens trying to buy some tat for second- and third-division friends. That's not my designation, by the way: this is how Radio 4 refers to such associates, and I'm not going to argue with Radio 4, am I? But why would you want to collect second- and third-division 'friends' in the first place? And why would you even contemplate buying a scented candle for Agnes, who is about to receive another fifty scented candles? Do you want her to burn the house down or something?

Apropos Agnes, I have another tale for you. During the Ice Age, when I was born, my parents left the registration of the happy event alarmingly late, so my dad was rather flustered when he arrived at the registry office just before the closing time. As he stands there panting, the registrar asks him the name of the newborn miracle.

To which he stumbles: "A... a... a..."

"Anna?" suggests the helpful official, keen to shut up shop and forget all about births, marriages and deaths for a little while.

"Anna!" confirms the relieved dad.

On returning home, he is greeted by the jubilant mum: "It's official now: we have our Agnieszka!" (Polish for Agnes.)

"Uhm... actually, sorry, no: it's Anna."

Talk about a lucky escape: I have been spared the hassle of having to spell my first name every time I utter it. I mean, in Britain. They also gave me an unpronounceable second name, but, of course, I don't use it – anything for an easy life. You would like to know what it is? 'Fraid not – it's between me and my tax inspector (yep, I do pay tax). But it certainly makes the job of impersonating me that bit harder. One of the few perks of being a foreigner in this wonderful country, I guess.

Returning to Christmas presents, Vinnie has embraced the Polish spirit of Yuletide, so we don't buy presents for friends, thereby sparing them from tit-for-tat gifting. Whoever put 'tat' into this adjective (which can also be used as a noun) seems to have had the right idea. So it's books for us and no tat for others. Granny certainly approves.

"A spiffing idea, lassie; books broaden the mind."

"They do, they do, Granny. And we actually say what books we want, so there are never any disappointments."

"Disappointments are best avoided, lassie. Life is full of them anyway, so there is no point in courting any unnecessary ones. Take all my late husbands, may they rest in peace. Each marriage started on a promising note, but things would soon go downhill," observed the senior of our clan with a reflective sigh. You see, like Elizabeth Taylor she was a serial marrier, having gone through seven husbands, although she had sufficient foresight not to marry any of them twice.

"No, there isn't, Granny. We have a lovely bookshop here in Keswick; it's called Bookends. You tell us what books you and Zdzislawa would like, we'll tell you what book each of us would like, and Bob's your uncle."

"And there won't be any unwanted presents!" jubilated Granny. "By the way, what do they do with all these unwanted gifts, lassie?"

"Oh, there is an entire industry for dealing with them."

"An entire *industry*? Actually, they did tell me that Britain was a highly industrialised country."

"Well, it's not this sort of industry, Granny. But they do write books about disposing of unwanted gifts."

"Blow me down! So what do these books say exactly?"

"Well, they describe all these different strategies."

"Such as?"

"They suggest you give unwanted presents to charity, recycle them, sell them, return them, throw a gift-swapping party…"

"*A gift-swapping party?*"

"Yep; they say you could actually organise a gift-swapping party."

"Isn't that more trouble than it's worth? Throwing good money after bad," mused Granny.

"Depends on whether you like parties, I suppose. Besides, people tend to get a bit low after Christmas, so a party might cheer them up."

"Why would people get a bit low after Christmas? *I* never do, lassie."

"No, neither do we, Granny, but think about it: you've been showered with unwanted gifts, you've put on half a stone – I mean three kilograms (Poland is fully metric, but, thanks to Brexit, Britain might soon be freed from the tyranny of the metric system; at least that's what the government had promised the electorate) – you've pickled your liver, you've taken your decorations down, you've got into debt, you've…"

"You've got *into debt*? *Whyever* would you get into debt?"

"Think about it: you've spent all this money on presents, and…"

"You go into debt *buying presents*?"

"People do, yes. Do you know that they spend billions of pounds on Christmas gifts every year? It's part of British culture."

Granny looked utterly flabbergasted. "This British culture takes some working out, lassie. Are you saying that, after they've spent billions of pounds on Christmas gifts, they then have to buy books that tell them how to get rid of those gifts?"

"Well, not *all* of those gifts – only two billion pounds' worth."

"*Only?*"

"I know, I know. But there is also another strategy."

"Another strategy? What's that?"

"Starting a bad-present pool."

"A *bad-present pool*?"

"Yep. These books suggest you get together with like-minded friends or colleagues, put all your bad presents into a sack, then fish them out at random and have a jolly good chuckle."

"Isn't that a bit mean, child?"

"Maybe a bit, but it's better than just dumping your unwanted presents in the bin, I suppose."

"Do people do this?"

"Oh yes; in this country, some 15 million people throw unwanted presents straight into the bin."

"*Fifteen million* people? Blow me down."

"I know, Granny, I know. That's exactly why we've resolved to avoid all this insanity with *our* Christmas presents."

Both Granny and Zdzislawa having, for quite a while, cogitated on this particular aspect of British culture in silence, the four of us went shopping. The book buying was a piece of cake, and we soon had all our *wanted* presents sorted. But I also needed to purchase some more festive food; after all, I would now be catering for four (which, by the way, is the maximum my mental health can withstand). Thankfully, we have good shops in Keswick.

"Are we having carp on Christmas Eve?" enquired Granny, surveying the fish counter with an expectant eye. We had reached our excellent supermarket, Booths, and started filling up the trolley. No, not one of those gigantic ones – just a standard size – and we were not anticipating constructing a pyramid on top of it either.

"No, they don't do carp in Britain."

"*They don't do carp*? So how can they celebrate Christmas Eve properly?"

"They don't celebrate Christmas Eve at all, Granny."

"*They don't celebrate Christmas Eve?* Pull the other one!"

"Honestly, Granny, they don't. But don't worry: *we* will. It will have to be with a different fish, though. And something nice and veggie for you, darling," I quickly added, offering my young vegan cousin what I hoped was an eco-friendly smile. I must say I was a bit worried by her subduedness, but it's probably a phase she was going through. That's what happens when you are young. Apparently. Or maybe she was still traumatised by the wrong type of snow and all the strikes. Vinnie was also being taciturn, but I was well used to this facet of his personality. Do you know how many words per day are uttered by an average man? Seven thousand. And by an average woman? Twenty thousand. But Vinnie is far from an average man, anyway: his daily output hovers around the five-hundred mark (if that). This is why I can never drag much out of him on his return from the pub or from wherever else he has been socialising with his friends.

"So what did you talk about?" I would enquire.

"Oh, this and that."

"Such as?"

"Nothing really."

"But you were gone five hours. You *must* have talked about something."

"Oh, I don't know; just chit-chat."

At which point, I helpfully suggest that, next time, perhaps we could fit him with a voice recorder or something. Regrettably, he fails to see the funny side, so that's that.

Before I get on with the story, I feel I owe you an explanation vis-à-vis Granny's colourful language. Whenever they visit us, both she and Zdzislawa, who, like me, are ardent Anglophiles, are extremely keen to practise their English and insist on using it even when they speak to me. Besides, they wouldn't dream of communicating with me in Polish in Vinnie's presence – that's impeccable breeding for you. Such breeding is not confined to the West, you see. And Granny in particular is very hot on all sorts of lively colloquialisms, which she, understandably, cannot pick up in Poland, even though English is the most popular foreign language in the country. But there are limits. This is why she is always asking me and Vinnie to teach her colourful expressions. We do oblige – hence her 'blow me downs', 'pull the other ones' and suchlike, which she delights in using whenever an appropriate opportunity presents itself.

18

Murder in the Bath, Foxtrot with Charlie, English Grammar, Monoglots and Tranquillity

"Do you remember how we used to buy fish in times gone by?" reminisced Granny. "They would deliver all these live fish and put them in these huge water-filled tanks."

"I do, I do, Granny, but I was very young then. I do remember that they would wrap a live fish in paper for my mum, and she would carry it home in a bag dripping with water all the way."

"Oh no! Poor fish; that's so vile." Zdzislawa winced with an utmost distaste. Well, at least she finally spoke (in English, as always), so that was something.

"Well, that's how it was in those days, child. You then kept it in the bath."

"Why would you keep it in the bath?" enquired the girl.

"Because we had no fridge."

"So how did you bathe?"

"We didn't – not until we despatched the fish."

"Where did you despatch it to?"

"To carp heaven, lassie."

"*What?*"

"I meant… you know… killed."

"Oh, n-o-o-o!" wailed Zdzislawa, raising her hands to her temple in a gesture of utter exasperation. Passionate about animals, she was apparently very active in the Polish animal rights movement. It must run in families – even the extended ones – this love of animals.

"Well, that's how it was in those days."

"So how did you… did you… do it, Nana?"

"Well, it was the job for the husband *du jour*. Take Wawrzyniec, may he rest in peace, for example. He would usually whack it with something."

"Oh, n-o-o, barbarians, murderers, *killers!*" screamed Zdzislawa, shaking her head violently and burying it in her hands.

"'S everyfynk aw wight, madam?"

I quickly turned round and saw a burly gentleman shooting my young cousin an investigative look.

"It's just a little misunderstanding," I reassured him with a nervous laugh, which I hoped didn't sound too pathetic.

"If you don' mind, I were speakin' to the young lass, like – *police*." On seeing my baffled expression – he wasn't in uniform – he smugly added, "Off duty, like – but *never* off the scent."

"O-o-o-o, they killed… killed…" sobbed Zdzislawa, whose distress was palpable.

"Charlie – Uniform – Foxtrot –Tango, I need them reinforcements sharpish: suspected muider; they look like them East Europeans," barked the man into his walkie-talkie – or whatever the thingy was – which he had suddenly procured from somewhere about his person. At that point, a small group of onlookers started gathering around us, and I was beginning to panic.

"No, no, Officer, it's not…"

"Killed… killed in the… in the bath," howled my young cousin.

"Stay where yous are: I arrest yous on suspicion of muider," snarled the bloke, looking at Granny and me balefully. "Yous don' need to say anyfynk, but it may 'arm your defence…"

"No, no, Officer, *we didn't kill anybody!*"

"Thas *not* what the young lass seems to be allegin', like."

"In the bath!" wailed Zdzislawa.

The man moved closer to her. "Was you sayin' the body is still in the baf?"

I was now desperate. "No, no, no, Officer, *there is no body!*"

He looked at me with deep suspicion. "Yous disposed of it, like?"

"No, no, no, *no*: she means *fish!*"

"*What* fish?"

"Christmas carp."

"There's no such species – I know 'bout them fishes: I done lotsa anglin', like."

"No, no, I mean carp *for* Christmas – it's traditional."

"We 'ave *turkey* at Christmas, madam – like all them civilised people, like."

"No, no, I mean *in Poland*."

"Yous Polish?"

"Yes, Officer. We always have carp on Christmas Eve."

"And mushroom soup," whispered Granny, clearly determined to hold her own regardless.

"On them British benefits, I take it." The man smirked. "All them immigrants must be laughin'."

"No, no, Officer, *nobody* is on benefits – I have *always* worked hard. And paid my taxes; I'm a writer; I write about grammar."

"Who'd wanna read 'bout Polish grammar, like?"

"No, no, not Polish grammar: *English* grammar."

"You're 'avin' me on, like: English don't 'ave no grammar."

"It does, Officer; it has plenty of grammar – practically oodles. I find it fascinating; it's my great…"

"And poppy seed cake," muttered Granny, clearly stuck in the Christmas Eve groove. "Christmas wouldn't be the same without poppy seed cake."

The man, whose hearing must have been superior to that of the tiger moth, turned towards Granny.

"S'that what yous do to get 'igh, madam?"

"I think it's 'to get *me*' – not 'to get *I*'," murmured Granny. I have to say that I was impressed by her grasp of English grammar but needed to correct her nevertheless.

"He means 'to get *high*', Granny."

"O-o-o," reflected Granny, "we use a ladder."

"*What* ladder?" barked the man.

"The aluminium one; it extends, so you can get quite high."

"I meant *for kicks*, like."

"But we *don't* kick, Officer. The only time I had to kick my Mieczyslaw, may he rest in peace, was when he wouldn't stop snoring, but…"

"I suggest you stop takin' the mick, madam, or this wiw be took as an aggravatin' factor in your crime, like."

"No, no, Officer, my granny… she doesn't realise you meant opium."

"She *don't* realise?"

"No, Officer, we've never done drugs – *ever*. In any case, you don't trip on poppy seed cake. And her idiomatic English does let her down every now and then."

The sleuth nodded sagely. "Them immigrants, they should learn to speak proper like what we do, like."

"But *neither* of them lives here, Officer; they just came to visit my husband and me. After Christmas, they will be travelling to Florida. If there are no more strikes. The right type of snow would also help. And we are just doing a bit of Christmas shopping now."

"After yous done the muider?"

"*There was no murder, Officer*! We were just telling my cousin that, decades ago, we'd buy live carp for Christmas and then have to… to kill it at home."

"After yous gave it a baf, like?"

"No, no, we kept it in the bath simply because we didn't have a fridge."

The man scratched his head, loosened his shirt collar and turned to my young cousin.

"S'that true, madam?"

Zdzislawa, her face still buried in her hands, continued sobbing, seemingly unaware of the whole hubbub.

"Madam, s'this true?" persisted the sleuth.

"Is... is... what... what true?"

"That you meant fish, like."

"Of... of course... of course I meant... I meant fi... fish. So... so cruel; ani... animals, they... they deserve to be... to be trea... treated the same... the same as hu... humans; they are... are li... living thi... things, they fee... feel the... feel the pa... pain the same... the same as... as u... u... us."

The bloke, now looking somewhat discombobulated, cleared his throat, raised the walkie-talkie thingy to his lips again and said into it: "Charlie – Uniform – Foxtrot –Tango, crime cleared up; stand them reinforcements down."

"Are we free to go, Officer?" I pleaded, although rather more weakly than I would have liked.

"Uhrm, yous are, like," said the guy, who then executed a swift 180-degree turn and proceeded hurriedly towards condiments, spices and pickles. For a brief moment, I wondered if he was going to get himself some sauerkraut and if he had ever tried bigos. It's traditional Polish fare; you make it with sauerkraut. Maybe you could try it some time. For example, for your ethnic evening or something. Britain does this sort of thing rather well: after all, it is a welcoming place. Apart from the recalcitrant cyclist who told me to bugger off to my own country (I know, I know, I've already told you about him – several times – but my memory of this incident is stuck in my mind like Common Burdock: I simply cannot get rid of it).

But back to our unfortunate incident. The crowd started dispersing – albeit somewhat reluctantly, with some people continuing to look at us over their shoulder as they toddled off. Don't forget that our wonderful supermarket attracts a refined clientele: I've already told you that they call it a high-end one. Can you imagine what would have happened in a low-end outfit? It doesn't bear thinking about. They might have even called *The Sun* for an exclusive.

"Shall we go and get some coffee and cake, lassie? My nerves are shot."

"Good idea, Granny." We gently steered the still inconsolable Zdzislawa towards the supermarket café.

"The British police, they are very vigilant, aren't they? Even when they are off duty," reflected Granny over a rum baba. It must have been particularly rich, for it gave off an intoxicating vapour.

"They are, Granny, they are; their crime clear-up rates are quite impressive: nearly eight per cent, I think."

"I'm not at all surprised, lassie: he said he'd cleared this one up – although there was no crime in the first place." The old lady smacked her lips. "This rum baba, it has a real bite – not like Jack Daniel's."

Those supermarket people must be weathering the cost-of-living crisis pretty well if they can afford to infuse their cakes with such copious amounts of alcohol, I reflected. But maybe the cost-of-living crisis doesn't affect supermarkets… particularly the high-end ones?

"I think I might switch to rum," continued Granny. "I've heard that this Mount Gay Special Reserve is particularly potent: at my time of life, one needs all the help one can get. Why do you think he wanted to go dancing, lassie?"

"*Dancing*, Granny?"

"Yes, with Charlie."

"Who's Charlie?"

"I don't know, do I? The one in the uniform, I presume."

"*What* uniform?"

"Charlie's, I presume. I could never resist a uniform. My Tomasz, may he rest in peace, he looked exceedingly handsome in his."

"Yes, Granny, a smart uniform has a certain *je ne sais quoi* – no two ways about it. But what has a uniform got to do with this guy – this policeman? *If* he was a policeman, that is. He wasn't wearing a uniform of any sort. And some folk like pretending they are something they are not."

"No, no, not *him*. It sounded to me as if he fancied some foxtrot and tango with this uniformed Charlie."

"Oh, Granny – ha, ha, ha!"

"I must admit I also thought it was a bit funny, lassie. Why would you even *contemplate* dancing when you have all those villains to catch? I mean *real* villains."

"No, no, Granny! It's just… ha, ha, ha… it's just the police alphabet."

"The *police alphabet*? Do the police have their own alphabet here? I was under the impression that you used the Latin alphabet in Britain; are you saying that it's too difficult for the police to get their head around? Mind you, the way he was speaking…"

"No, no, Granny; they use a special word for each letter to avoid confusion over the airwaves. So, for example, Alpha is for A…"

"*Of course*, alpha is for A, lassie – that's exactly what I mean by the Latin alphabet."

"No, Granny, this is different. For B, they use Bravo, for C, Charlie, for D, Delta and so on and so forth."

"You mean foxtrot is for F and tango for T?"

"Spot on, Granny. And Uniform is for U. He was probably using these letters as some sort of code."

"I s-e-e-e," mused the senior of our clan as she continued to annihilate the rum baba. "But why did he say that English had no grammar?"

"Probably because they had stopped teaching grammar in the late sixties and then kept it off the school curriculum until they came to their senses in the noughties."

"Pull the other one: grammar underpins all communication!" exclaimed the old lady in utter amazement.

"I know, I know, Granny, but they reckoned that grammar stifled creativity."

"So did they become more creative when they stopped teaching grammar?"

"Well, accountants seem to have done, Granny."

"Accountants, lassie?"

"Yes, Granny, I understand there is a lot of creative accounting going on. They capitalise on loopholes in accounting laws and regulations. To make companies look more successful and profitable than they actually are."

"*In Britain?* I didn't think they did things like this, lassie. Just as well that they started teaching grammar again."

"Just as well, Granny. But they might have taught grammar in public schools throughout."

"What do you mean – aren't all schools public?"

"No, no, Granny: in Britain, public schools are private schools."

"You mean all schools in Britain are *private*, lassie? But you said they *hadn't* taught grammar!"

"No, no, Granny, they might have taught grammar in public, I mean private, schools, but only about seven per cent of kids attend such schools."

"So where do the rest go?"

"To state schools. Largely."

"I s-e-e-e," mused Granny. "So are you saying that only seven per cent of pupils were taught English grammar here?"

"Well, until the noughties – probably. It's now back on the school curriculum, though. But think about it: some teachers hadn't been taught grammar themselves, so how are they supposed to do a competent job of teaching their pupils? This is why I have written a grammatical textbook – to help them. It's called *Grammar and Punctuation for Key Stages 3 & 4 with Handy Usage Notes*."

"What are Key Stages 3 and 4, lassie?"

"Essentially, the whole of secondary school, spanning the ages from eleven to sixteen. But the book can also be used by A-level and university students and adults generally. It's very accessible and has plenty of examples; some of them are really funny."

"Why are they funny, lassie?"

"Well, people don't mean for them to be funny, but, when you don't know grammar, you are far more likely to make grammatical and punctuation mistakes, and some of them are unintentionally hilarious – just like those dangling participles. I've been showing you my articles and books on dangling participles, don't you remember?"

"Oh yes, all those disintegrated investigators, sliced cars, childbearing boyfriends and destructive weather forecasters – ha, ha, ha!"

"Well remembered, Granny. Teachers have been saying that my textbook is really helpful."

"That's good, lassie; helpful things are very good for your blood pressure. Take my divorces, for example: I felt so much better after each one. But what happens with foreign languages here? Obviously, when you are studying a foreign language, you have to learn its grammar."

"Obviously, Granny, but learning a foreign language beyond the age of fourteen hasn't been compulsory in England since 2004, and the subject is declining in popularity. Only forty per cent of students now take it at GCSE."

"What's GCSE, lassie?"

"It's an exam taken by pupils at the age of sixteen. And only a minority of Britons can converse in a foreign language. I think it's less than forty per cent – the lowest proportion in Europe. Quite a few expect English to be spoken in whatever country they visit, you know."

"I know, I know, lassie. Whenever I bump into British tourists in Warsaw, they always shout and wave their arms about. But they are very pleased when I reply in English."

"Funny you should say that, Granny: I have written a ditty about it; would you like to hear it?"

"Very much, lassie."

The language in Spain?
No good for the brain:
No clue what they're talking about;
We're proud monoglots,
We like English – lots,
You speak our tongue, or we shout.

On hearing *adieu*,
We sulk and we stew:
Those Frogs are as bad as they seem;
We're proud monoglots,
We like English – lots,
You speak our tongue, or we scream.

In Tokyo, a Jap,
A pleasant old chap,
Says something, but one's in the dark;
We're proud monoglots,
We like English – lots,
You speak our tongue, or we bark.

What's all this about
When some ginger Kraut
Jumps up and starts shouting *schnell*, *schnell*?
We're proud monoglots,
We like English – lots,
You speak our tongue, or we yell.

> In Warsaw, a Pole,
> On calling the roll,
> Goes: "Welcome, your bags are just there;"
> This pleases us – lots
> (We're proud monoglots),
> But why can't they *all* be like her?

Granny nodded. "Yes, all our kids have to learn at least one foreign language at school. Until they are eighteen. But they usually take two. Learning foreign languages makes you open to other cultures. How many did you study, child?"

"Two. And Latin as an extra," replied Zdzislawa, rubbing her eyes, still very red after all the crying.

"Dead as a dodo, though," observed the senior of my clan.

"But Latin is so logical, Granny: I also took it. All this fantastic grammar – I loved it!"

Another three rum babas later, Granny managed to steady her nerves to a sufficient degree to resume shopping. Admittedly, Zdzislawa remained somewhat unsettled, but Granny offered her ample reassurances that the despatching of the carp would have been carried out in as humane a manner as possible. And this was no longer happening, of course: everybody had a fridge now – even in Poland. Do any of you remember the pre-fridge days? I do. Talk about poverty. Everything is relative, I guess…

Anyway, we managed to stock up on our Christmas essentials – minus the carp, instead of which we would have steamed wild salmon, my specialty (how did you guess?). And vegan tikka masala for Zdzislawa; it came ready-made in a packet, and I can just about cope with that. But we'd also have heaps of vegetables – steamed, of course – as well as fruit, nuts and seeds: no nutritional deficiency under our roof. This healthy-eating habit of mine was formed way back in Poland: we might have all been equally poor under communism (apart from party apparatchiks, that is), but we didn't have any of this junk, highly-processed, stuff. An interesting case of poverty working in your favour.

Back home, Granny, clearly exhausted by the whole hoo-ha and knocked out by the rum babas, soon nodded off while Vinnie, Zdzislawa and I put our shopping away. Into the fridge, which even has a freezer compartment! The three of us then had some organic kefir (very good for your gut bacteria) before Zdzislawa and I sat down to watch a documentary on predators in Africa. No, not the Wagner Group mercenaries – things like lions, leopards and cheetahs. I've told you that Zdzislawa loves animals, even if they are of the killing variety, but she accepts that it's just nature. Which the human race thinks it can mess with – with impunity. But it can't. Vinnie, meanwhile, went off to watch some match on another TV set. Incidentally, would you like to know a recipe for an enduring and harmonious marriage? Separate bedrooms, separate bathrooms and separate TV sets. That's the only recipe I know, by the way, but it works.

Now, hold this scene in your mind's eye: outside, the snow – of the right variety this time – is gently falling, whereas, inside, our miniature plastic Christmas tree adds a festive touch to the mantlepiece, the reindeer figurine nestles contentedly on the bookshelf, and the cut-price tinsel adorns two picture frames. And, all the while, the flickering gas fire is making strenuous, though not entirely convincing, efforts to affect a semblance to the real thing. Meanwhile Granny is snoring melodiously on the sofa, and the three of us are engrossed in our respective TV programmes. In other words, all is peace, albeit occasionally punctuated by Vinnie's hollers: "Come on, son! That was *never* offside! Take the ball – *not* the man!" Those desperate yelps notwithstanding, I sincerely hope I have managed to invoke a picture of serenity here. It was certainly my intention, my understanding being that, for the native population, Christmas is by far the most stressful time of the year. More stressful than a bereavement, divorce and house move combined. And multiplied by ten. I really can't understand why one of the popular Christmas songs wishes that it was Christmas every day – *really?* Tranquillity is thus the note on which I would like to finish this book. There just remain my warm season's greetings to convey to you all – provided somebody is actually reading this book, but Christmas is supposed to be the time of hope for all mankind. Unless you celebrate Diwali, Ashura, Eid, Holi, Ramadan or Baptism of Muhammad, that is.

> At this special time of year,
> Let me raise a Yuletide cheer:
> Merry Christmas to you all,
> Just relax and have a ball
> And, to say the very least,
> Most delicious festive feast;
> But, though tipple is no sin,
> Do go easy on the gin!